# GOD HAS AN APP FOR THAT!

Many grew up never understanding the connection of their faith to everyday life. Sunday seemed completely irrelevant to Monday. This powerful book shows the life-change that takes place when Scripture is applied. *God Has an App for That!* both encourages and challenges readers to live out God's Word. Dudley skillfully combines biblical information with practical application, which I believe will cause the reader to experience lasting transformation.

**Kyle Idleman,** Teaching Pastor, Southeast Christian Church
Louisville, Kentucky (www.southeastchristian.org)

*God Has an App for That!* provides real world wisdom and meaning in the midst of the high-speed digital age in which we live. It is a must-read for anyone who desires to grow in the Christian faith. This book will help you find God's perfect app for just about any obstacle you may be facing today!

**Scott Brooks,** Head Coach, Oklahoma City Thunder (www.nba.com/thunder/)

In a culture in which a myriad of technological tools claim to make one's life easier, this book successfully proves that the Word of God is the true source of relevant answers for today's believer. With the same ease that one would download an app to a smartphone, Dudley Rutherford guides the reader through practical and biblical steps to achieving victory in many areas of life. I have no doubt that reading *God Has an App for That!* will be an important milestone in the lives of Christian men and women everywhere.

**Charles E. Blake,** Presiding Bishop, Church of God in Christ
Senior Pastor, West Angeles Church of God in Christ
Los Angeles, California (www.esta.org)

My friend Dudley has written a masterpiece of practical wisdom from a biblical perspective that will transform your life. It's simple, relevant and effective! This is one of those treasures that under-promises and over-delivers!

**Dale C. Bronner,** Author and Senior Pastor, Word of Faith Family Worship Cathedral, Atlanta, Georgia (www.woffamily.org)

In a rapidly changing, distracted and disrupted world, *God Has an App for That!* is a brilliant reminder that God's message of hope cuts through the clutter and reaches us all—if we'll just stop and listen. Dudley Rutherford gets today's culture, and this book is a brilliant answer.

**Phil Cooke,** Filmmaker and Media Consultant (www.philcooke.com)
Author, *Jolt: Get the Jump on a World That's Constantly Changing*

In *God Has an App for That!* Pastor Dudley Rutherford brilliantly brings the timeless wisdom of the Bible to life in the context of apps to show you that whatever your situation, God has an app to heal, educate and encourage you! A brilliant must-read.

**Thomas N. Ellsworth,** Co-founder, Premier Digital Publishing
Former CEO, GoTV Networks

Helpful. Insightful. Relevant. If you are searching for assistance to help you through some of life's problems, then *God Has An App for That!* Every person at some point of life needs what this book has to offer. Get it. Read it. Share it.

**Ronnie W. Floyd,** Senior Pastor, Cross Church, Northwest Arkansas
(www.crosschurch.com); Author, *Our Last Great Hope*

Allow me to begin by saying that you should read everything Dudley Rutherford writes! He is a most exceptional and insightful pastor—one of the most anointed I have met. In *God Has an App for That!* he brings the book of James to life and provides real answers to the biggest obstacles you may encounter in your Christian walk. If you have searched for lasting solutions in our fast-paced, technologically advanced world, you will not be disappointed by this wonderful book. Become immersed in God's apps and find encouragement and enrichment for your soul!

**Jim Garlow,** Senior Pastor, Skyline Wesleyan Church
San Diego, California (www.skylinechurch.org)

If you're up to "alert, alive, creative and on target," you're ready for Dudley Rutherford. But be sure of this: He's about what's real, not only what's up. And when he talks about God, you are hearing about God's heart from a trustworthy shepherd of souls! I urge you to connect with him—and this book is a great way to start.

**Jack W. Hayford,** President, The King's University, Van Nuys, California
(www.kingsuniversity.edu)

I have known Dudley Rutherford for the past 10 years and have been greatly influenced, inspired and challenged by his ministry. Based on timeless principles found in the book of James, this book will cause your love for God to deepen and compel you to becoming the person He has created you to be. Enjoy downloading these relevant and practical truths, and then experience the blessings they bring to your life.

**Kevin Jordan,** Team Chaplain, Pittsburgh Steelers (http://thejordanreport.org/)

If you, like me, are looking for smart ways to dig out from the avalanche of daily "got-to's," "have-to's" and "need to's," then this is the book for you. It's not one more thing to add to some list—it's the thing that will help you strategically eliminate the noise in your list so you can focus on what's really important . . . and, ultimately, eternal. Because, as Dudley says, "God has an app for that."

**Frank Pastore,** Host, *The Frank Pastore Show* (www.frankpastore.com)

*God Has an App for That!* is filled with help for life's dilemmas. Dudley shares downloadable directions that can transform your life. Apply them today!

**Dave Stone,** Senior Minister, Southeast Christian Church
Louisville, Kentucky (www.southeastchristian.org)

Pastor Dudley Rutherford is uniquely gifted in finding the profundity in simplicity and making it simplistically profound. *In God Has an App for That!* he addresses some of the tough issues common to all of us with relevant revelations of practical truth. His scholarship is so effectively woven within the fabric of practicality that you will be unaware that you are on a journey of positive change until you realize your spiritual hard drive has been reprogrammed with eternal truth. Put this work on your homepage, click the icon on your wallpaper, and expect God to upgrade your life!

**Kenneth C. Ulmer,** Senior Pastor/Teacher, Faithful Central Bible Church
Los Angeles, California (www.faithfulcentral.com)
Past President, The King's University
Presiding Bishop, Macedonia International Bible Fellowship

We all face challenges, and we all have issues. In his practical, easy-to-read style, Dudley has written a book that can help everyone! We loved the stories and the clear biblical direction. God really does have an app for every part of our life, so pick up this great book for yourself and your friends!

**Philip and Holly Wagner**
Co-pastors, Oasis Church, Los Angeles, California (www.oasisla.org)

Pastor Dudley is a visionary leader/teacher who has availed his life to advancing God's kingdom and His people in the most innovative ways. In a time where so many are faced with inexplicable challenges, this timely book reminds us that God, in His incomprehensible love for us all, "has an app for that." I've downloaded the app . . . and now I'm ready and armed to skillfully use it.

**Danita Patterson,** Writer and Award-winning Producer
Founder, Destiny Unlimited, Inc. and Destiny Outreach, Inc.

Dudley brings years of insight and wisdom to major life issues we all face. *God Has an App for That!* is full of helpful content and life-changing application. This is an awesome, practical guide for the real stuff of life. Highly recommended!

**Jud Wilhite,** Senior Pastor, Central Christian Church, Las Vegas, Nevada
(www.centralchristian.com); Author, *Torn* and *Throw It Down*

James has always been one of my favorite authors in the Bible because he doesn't just ask, "So what?" but he says, "Now what?" Dudley Rutherford gets that, and in this book he will help you to get it too. Take *God Has an App for That!* out for a test drive. You are apt to be blessed!

**Rick Atchley,** The Hills Church of Christ, North Richland Hills, Texas
(www.thehills.org)

There is something very special about the way Dudley relays a message. It just makes sense. I read this book during a two-hour drive to Barstow, and I couldn't put it down. It is a must-read for Generation X and Y, who undoubtedly are searching for spiritual answers in this advanced and ever-changing world.

**Patrick Bet-David,** Founder, People Helping People Financial Services
Los Angeles, California

# God Has an App for That!

Discover God's Solutions for the Major Issues of Life

# DUDLEY
# RUTHERFORD

**Regal**

**From Gospel Light**
**Ventura, California, U.S.A.**

Published by Regal
From Gospel Light
Ventura, California, U.S.A.
*www.regalbooks.com*
Printed in the U.S.A.

Library of Congress Cataloging-in-Publication Data
Rutherford, Dudley.
  God has an app for that : discover God's solutions for the major issues of life / Dudley Rutherford.
      p. cm.
  Includes bibliographical references and index.
  ISBN 978-0-8307-6088-6 (hardcover : alk. paper)
  1. Christian life I. Title.
  BV4501.3.R887 2012
  248.4—dc23
2011033353

Rights for publishing this book outside the U.S.A. or in non-English languages are administered by Gospel Light Worldwide, an international not-for-profit ministry. For additional information, please visit www.glww.org, email info@glww.org, or write to Gospel Light Worldwide, 1957 Eastman Avenue, Ventura, CA 93003, U.S.A.

To order copies of this book and other Regal products in bulk quantities, please contact us at 1-800-446-7735.

*In honor of the wisest person*
*I have ever had the privilege of knowing personally,*
**Coach John R. Wooden,**
*who once said,*
*"You can't live a perfect day without doing something for someone who will never be able to repay you."*

# Contents

**Acknowledgments**................................................................................11

**Introduction:** God Has an App for Your Every Need .................................13

# God Has an App to …

▶ 1. Turn Stress into Joy ...........................................................25

▶ 2. Overcome Temptation........................................................49

▶ 3. Break Down the Walls that Divide.........................................73

▶ 4. Resuscitate a Dying Faith....................................................91

▶ 5. Curb Your Profanity ..........................................................111

▶ 6. Restore a Broken Heart .....................................................131

▶ 7. Prioritize Your Investments ................................................153

▶ 8. Heal Your Affliction ...........................................................175


**Conclusion**.........................................................................................197

**Appendix A:** God Has an App to Help You Find
Encouragement in the Bible .................................................201

**Appendix B:** God Has an App to Take You Through the Bible
in One Year.........................................................................203

**Endnotes**..........................................................................................209

# Acknowledgements

From cover to cover, this book is the combined effort of so many gifted individuals who deserve to be recognized and appreciated. First and foremost, I want to thank the Regal publishing house family who took all my dreams for this project and turned them into reality. We knew that, with the explosion of new technology and available phone apps springing onto the market, there was a timing issue that required "all hands on deck." And with Regal's professional expertise and heart to see the world impacted for the Lord, this book was made possible.

Next, I must express my gratitude to three people who helped craft so much of this book, starting with my beautiful daughter, Kayla, who is gifted beyond her years. I am a blessed father to have such a talented daughter who loves the Lord and is willing to help wherever needed. My brilliant writing assistant, Angela Merrill, who is really an angel in disguise, carried the most responsibility in the execution of this book, working as the liaison between Regal and me and meeting all the development deadlines that seem to approach with lightning speed. Finally, Kyle Welch, who might be the smartest person I have ever met, actually convinced me that he enjoyed working on this project and so wonderfully created inspiring content.

Doing an injustice by listing their names alphabetically, I want to thank Rhona Cue (editing), Deena Davis (copyeditor), Steve Lawson (senior editor), Mark Weising (managing editor) and Rob Williams (designer). This team created a synergy that truly helped this book reach its full potential.

Finally, at a very young age I was taught the value of knowing God's Word. I want to thank my parents and all the teachers, coaches, fellow church members, professors and mentors who came alongside me at some point of life's journey to teach me God's truth. It was in hearing the Scriptures that I first fell in love with God and discovered that the Bible was actually a love letter from Him to us. This book came from the burden I have for you to discover the enlightening truth and application from the greatest book ever written . . . the Bible.

# Introduction

## God Has an App for Your Every Need

Sometimes in the middle of the night, a pesky intruder interrupts my much-needed slumber. I wish it were as simple as a buzzing fly in my bedroom or an incessant car alarm in the neighborhood, but the intruder is none other than my own thoughts and concerns. I find myself awake at 3 A.M., suddenly thinking about the pressures at work—an upcoming speaking engagement, a meeting or an impending project deadline. Other times, I am consumed by the natural burdens a parent has for his or her children.

In the midst of these bouts of occasional insomnia, I often pray or stare enviously at my beautiful wife who is sleeping soundly. Then, conceding the fact that I'm probably *not* going to fall back to sleep, I consider getting out of bed and going to the state-of-the-art gym down the street or shuffling downstairs to catch an NBA game I recorded earlier, while fast-forwarding through all the commercials. The thought even crosses my mind to run over to Denny's for breakfast, since it's open 24 hours a day. (Probably not as wise a choice as working out, but you have to admit, a Grand Slam is always appealing.) In our fantastically fast-paced world of cool conveniences, almost any service or necessity is available around the clock.

As I toss and turn in bed, what usually happens is that I don't take advantage of any of the above-mentioned options. Instead, I reach over to my nightstand, grab my smartphone and look at my emails, text messages, calendar, Twitter, Facebook, blog, and so on. My mind gets so saturated with more ideas, concerns and to-do lists that it's impossible to return to a sleep mode. That's when I wish I could turn off all of these worries and get back to sleep, so that I won't be exhausted and ill-prepared for the hectic schedule that awaits me in just a few hours. I need an app for that!

After all, smartphones, smart cars, gadgets, widgets and apps are designed to make our lives simpler, aren't they? As I write, we are rapidly approaching 1 million applications available for mobile phones and tablets,[1] and more than 15 billion individual apps have been downloaded through Apple alone.[2] There are apps to help you find where you parked your car and apps that allow you to scan a product and find the best deal. There's an app that analyzes the local weather to determine how it will affect your hair[3] and one that enables you to take out your frustrations by flinging angry birds at green piglets that have a penchant for stealing eggs.[4]

With so many practical (and some purely whimsical) technological aids to make life easier (or emotionally cathartic) why do so many people still hurt or feel stressed, afraid, discontent and unfulfilled? Whenever an ailment or deficiency of the mind, body or heart gets our attention, we're quick to hop on the Internet and search for the best cyber remedy. I just typed in the word "self-help" on Google's homepage and received 117,000,000 results in .14 seconds! That's a lot of answers. But if Internet results, apps, blogs, Tweets or texts truly possessed the answers to our ills, then why do problems and heartache still abound?

## Symptoms of the Struggle

Friend, it doesn't appear as though our knowledge or technological advances are making us happier, healthier or more harmonious people. Each year, 15 million adults suffer from clinical depression, and the number of people affected by this disorder increases each year.[5] Additionally, "the majority of Americans are living with moderate or high levels of stress, and while they understand that this is not healthy, they're stymied in their efforts to make changes."[6] Of 27,731 adults surveyed for a recent National Health Interview, 35 percent were overweight and 27 percent were obese.[7] It's not just our bodies that are under attack from without and within. Sadly, our relationships are also quite susceptible to trials and tribulations, as divorce claims 41 percent of first marriages, 60 percent of second marriages and 73 percent of third marriages in the U.S.[8] It breaks my heart to see so much suffering and hopelessness, knowing that there are so many in need of God's love and saving grace.

As a pastor in Los Angeles, the entertainment capital of the world, I'm always astonished to see certain celebrities who seem to have it all—a glamorous lifestyle, exciting career, exotic travels and the adulation of millions of fans—yet inevitably end up in the darkest, most deplorable of places. Rich or poor, black or white, young or old, no one is spared from the most vexing issues known to man.

Like a laboratory mouse scurrying from this point to that, with only little morsels of cheese to provide directional clues, we become exhausted as we attempt to make our way through the metaphorical maze of life. Despite so much available to us at the click of a button to inform, entertain, distract and amuse, so many of us are still confused, bored, stressed and lonely. We've desperately sought solutions to bring balance to our lives and alleviate our problems, but all to no avail.

## Looking for Answers in All the Wrong Places

*Maybe what I need is an expert,* you conclude, and so you sign up for countless hours of counseling sessions or watch a season of *Dr. Phil.* You might learn something by watching a TV program doling out sound advice, but with an overabundance of sources purporting to possess the right solution, too many people become confused as they try to navigate through life's rough waters.

Some people consult a daily horoscope, presuming that it's harmless enough (see 2 Chronicles 33:5-6 and Isaiah 47:13 for God's opinion about that). Others lose themselves in endless hours of watching television or playing video games, or they attempt to "live" vicariously through an alter ego in online virtual worlds.[9] An overwhelming number of people are looking for meaningful connections through Facebook—though this often turns into an unending competition to see who has the most "friends"!

The prevalence of our society's addictions to social media, alcohol, drugs, food, gambling or shopping is evidence that we are searching for answers in all the wrong places. Each year, in the United States, approximately 35,000 people choose to commit suicide as the ultimate remedy to their problems.[10] Friend, in our search for lasting solutions to life's deepest insufficiencies, we are looking everywhere but to the one place that has eternal answers, to the one place that's most obvious . . .

## An Untapped Treasure

Dr. Russell H. Conwell, an orator, lawyer and minister who lived in the late 1800s, traveled the United States telling a story that we are in dire need of hearing today.[11] It's a story about a man who owned a large farm near the Indus River in Southern Asia. The old farmer grew gardens, grain fields and orchards upon his lush land; but one day he heard about the immense wealth that could be gained through the diamond industry, and he was quite intrigued.

"With a handful of diamonds," an advisor told him, "you could purchase an entire country, and with a mine of diamonds, you could place your children on thrones!"

So he sold his farm, left his family in the care of a neighbor and embarked on a quest for the precious stones that were sure to make him unbelievably wealthy. But the search became protracted and painful. While traveling arduous miles through the valleys of the Himalayan Mountains, the deserts of Palestine and across the diverse terrain of Europe, the farmer continued to mine for the elusive diamonds and came up empty. Finally, standing on the shore of Barcelona, Spain—depressed, afflicted and penniless—he ended his life by casting himself into the violent incoming tide, never to be seen again.

Back home, the man who had purchased the farmer's land took his camel to the garden to drink one afternoon. When the camel dipped its nose into the transparent water of the shallow stream, the man noticed a strange flash of light coming from the sand. He reached down and extracted from the cool waters a dark stone possessing an eye of light that reflected all the colors of the rainbow. He carried it into the house, set it on the mantel and went on his way.

Sometime later, a visitor to the man's house noticed the curious pebble over the fireplace. He examined it and said, "This is a diamond!" The man replied, "No, it isn't. It's nothing but a stone I found right here in my garden."

Together, the two men ran to the garden and stirred up the sands of the brook with their hands and discovered other diamonds that were more beautiful and valuable than the first! Thus, the land sold by the poor old farmer became the diamond mines of Golconda, one of the richest diamond mines in the history of mankind.[12]

Do you want to know something intriguing? You have a treasure sitting in your own backyard. More likely, it's sitting on your coffee table or bookshelf, or in a closet or dusty box in the garage. This treasure is the Bible, the very words of God, which Psalm 19:10 describes as "more precious than gold" and Proverbs 8:11 depicts as "better than rubies" (*NKJV*), which speaks of its infinite worth.

"But, Dudley," you say, "the Bible is so old. It's too big; there are too many pages. And whenever I've tried to read it, I don't know where to start or how to get through it, so I just give up."

Well, my friend, let me break it down for you: There are 66 books within the Bible—39 books in the Old Testament and 27 books in the New Testament. (I know that may seem like a lot, but fiction authors John Grisham, J. K. Rowling and Danielle Steele have almost written just as many novels, and you've probably read them all, or ones like them!) The Old Testament records the origin and history of mankind, God's law, and a plethora of psalms to praise the Lord and bring comfort to people. The book of Proverbs imparts wisdom. The books of Isaiah, Jeremiah and Daniel reveal prophecy, and much more. The first four books of the New Testament are the Gospels, which record the life, death and resurrection of Jesus Christ. Letters to the early Christian churches, such as the 13 letters written by the apostle Paul, outline sound theological doctrine and encapsulate God's love and plan for humanity. The book of Revelation provides vivid imagery and details of the Last Days when God will judge the entire world during the final battle between good and evil, and the beginning of all things new when there will be a new heaven and a new earth, and God will make His dwelling place with man.

But of all the books in the Bible, the book of James is considered, without question, the most practical. It's a multifaceted jewel buried in the treasure of God's Word, offering practical solutions to everyday problems and a clear guide to Christian living. What's brilliant about the book of James is that you don't have to harness the IQ of an Albert Einstein or possess a theological degree to understand it. This book is for any person who is looking for direction and simplicity in this complicated world of ours.

If you are up against a perfect storm—struggling with any one or a combination of challenges such as stress, temptation, prejudice, a dying faith, profanity, a broken heart, materialism or any kind of physical affliction—you will discover God's peace-giving and life-changing response within His Word. It's as simple as a click of an icon in an app store. In fact, this is *the* app store of the Bible, and there is infinite power behind each topic we will examine.

Like putting a diving mask over your eyes during a scuba expedition and suddenly being able to see the resplendent colors of numerous varieties of fish and coral, God has an entire world He wants to reveal to you in His Word. Have you been in search of a buried treasure, like the diamonds of Golconda, to solve all your problems? Dear friend, most of us are not going to find great riches beneath the soil; but I promise that you will find something worth more than all the jewels on earth within the supernatural treasure of God's Word.

## Big-game James

Since we will be spending a considerable amount of time exploring God's apps that are located in the book of James, let's get acquainted with the author of this New Testament epistle.

Because James, the brother of Jesus (half-brother or stepbrother, to be accurate), had a front-row seat to the teaching, healing and miracles of God's Son, Jesus Christ, James is uniquely qualified to offer the spiritual answers to the questions that tug at our hearts. However, this close relative of Jesus may not always have been so spiritually discerning. When it came to accepting Christ as the Messiah, the Son of the Living God, John 7:5 tells us that "even his own brothers did not believe in him," and it is fair to assume that James was included in this assertion. But we read later, in 1 Corinthians 15:7, that Jesus appeared to James after the Resurrection. It is probably at this time that James became a believer. Next, we see James with his mother, family and the rest of the apostles in the upper room, waiting for the Holy Spirit (see Acts 1:14). By the time we get to Acts 12:17, James is in a church leadership position. He eventually became the lead pastor of the church at Jerusalem (see Acts 15:3).[13]

The opening of James's New Testament letter reveals an important detail that would fascinate even the casual reader. You'll notice that he elected to call himself "James, a *servant* . . . of the Lord Jesus Christ" (1:1, emphasis added), rather than "the brother of Jesus." That's pretty amazing to me. Imagine growing up with Jesus Christ, playing games and sitting at the dinner table with Him. If He was *your* brother, wouldn't you remind everyone of that fact via Twitter and Facebook . . . every day? But James didn't boast about it, as most of us would; instead, he chose to humble himself as a servant and exalt Jesus as his Lord.

As a true insider, with both humility and wisdom, James was able to address the most common issues with which we believers struggle, and he offers God's simple answers. Although he had never encountered an iPhone, BlackBerry or any other kind of smartphone, James understood that regardless of your circumstances—no matter what you might need—God has an app for that!

## Two Things Before We Get Started

As we dive into these apps, there are two critical principles that should motivate you to understand and "download" these apps found in the book of James:

### 1. God Cares About *Your* Problems

Yes! There are over 7 billion people on the planet today besides you,[14] but more impressive than that number is the fact that there is an all-powerful, all-knowing and ever-present God who actually cares about you—individually, personally and tenderly. His love for you is immeasurable, and He is specifically concerned about your troubles. In fact, He calls Himself your Father, Counselor, Comforter and Friend (see Isa. 9:6; Matt. 5:16,45; 6:9; John 15:14-15; Jas. 2:23).

*How do I know God cares for me?* you ask.

Well, not only did He take the time to create you along with our vast and stunning universe (see Gen. 1-2), but He also provides distinctly for you every day with food, shelter and clothing. Beyond daily provision, the Lord gives you the ability to experience relationships with others and, more importantly, to experience a personal relationship with Him. He created you with the strength to work, to receive satisfaction from your labor and to provide for your family. And by the way, children, spouses, parents, grandparents, siblings, aunts, uncles and cousins are also blessings from the Lord.

Unlike a person who abandons his or her child on the doorstep of a church or an orphanage, God, after creating us, didn't leave us here to wander around lost and confused. Instead, He gave us spiritual resources such as the Bible, which is His Word, and the Holy Spirit to guide us and comfort us in our deepest struggles. Moreover, He allows us to communicate with Him through prayer at any moment of the day! These are all benefits God bestows upon those who believe in Him and receive His gift of salvation through His Son, Jesus Christ.

In addition to showing you that He cares about you through the physical and spiritual blessings mentioned above, God *tells* you that He cares about you. Here is just one example from His Word: "Give all your worries and cares to God, for he cares about you" (1 Pet. 5:7, *NLT*). How awesome it is to know that the Creator of the universe is specifically concerned about your needs!

The ultimate proof of His love is that He made a provision for your salvation through the death of His one and only Son (see John 3:16). Jesus Christ shed His own blood as the atonement for our sins so that anyone who believes in Him can be forgiven, have a relationship with Him and live with Him forever in heaven. When was the last time you ever felt loved to that degree?

I'm sure there are a few people you can name who genuinely love you and express sympathy when you struggle, and try to help you. We naturally reach for and cling to any support we can grasp from others, but often we forget the unequivocal care and encouragement offered by the Lord God Himself. If you are weighed down by trials or heartache, don't run away from God; run *to* Him. No one loves you like He does (see Matt. 11:28).

Just a few years ago, I had the privilege of attending the NBA championship game in Los Angeles in which the L.A. Lakers competed against the Boston Celtics. I'll share more about this game in the next chapter, but for now, let me just tell you how surreal it was to sit among thousands and thousands of fans at the Staples Center during an exhilarating Game 7. The majority of the fans screamed and shouted their love and support for the Lakers. With exuberant devotion, they tirelessly chanted the players' names over and over. Some fans held up signs and banners displaying praise and encouragement. They did anything possible to spur on the athletes throughout the highs and lows of the performance.

Friend, do you realize this is one of the many roles God assumes in *your* life? He is your number-one fan! He enthusiastically cheers you on, desiring that you be victorious in all areas of your life so that you can fully glorify Him. God is inspiring, energizing, faithful, loyal, kind and reliable. He loves you, and He cares about your problems.

## 2. God Offers Life-changing Solutions to Your Problems

Not only is God aware of and concerned about your problems, but He also offers surefire answers to the most towering trials you may be facing today. Anyone can say he or she cares about you, but you need something more than just a verbal confirmation. You need someone who can step up to the plate and provide a solution, and that's exactly what God does. Job 12:13 asserts, "To God belong wisdom and power; counsel and understanding," and because He possesses these attributes, God is able to come alongside you and help you in your time of need.

If you were to take the cumulative value of every gadget, gizmo or guru on planet Earth, it still would not equal the incomparable power, wisdom, understanding and insight of the Lord God Almighty. Before there was Google, *God* possessed the answers to all your questions. And He still does. Look at what Jeremiah 33:2-3 affirms: "This is what the LORD says, he who made the earth, the LORD who formed it and established it—the LORD is his name: 'Call to me and I will answer you and tell you great and unsearchable things you do not know.'"

Why should you stumble around in the dark—bumping into walls or stubbing your toe on the corner of the dresser—as you search for a light switch in the middle of the night? Dear friend, this is exactly what we do when we turn anywhere other than to the Lord God for answers to life. King David, whom the Bible describes as a man after God's own heart (see 1 Sam. 13:13-14; Acts 13:22), understood that there is nothing on earth that can illuminate one's path like the Creator Himself. "You, LORD, are my lamp," David said. "The LORD turns my darkness into light" (2 Sam. 22:29).

Like a fiery torch piercing the blackest of nights, God's apps shed light on the most difficult dilemmas that confront us. When you are seeking truth, salvation, joy, peace, why search anywhere else but the one, true Source for every solution? Our Father in heaven knows everything, even the depths of our hearts (see 1 John 3:20), and it is His desire that we come to Him alone when we need deliverance from a particular sin, problem or predicament.

Reading this book is an excellent step toward some important changes in your spiritual growth. Whether you are battling to remain faithful to what you truly value in a culture in which trials and temptations abound—or if you are discouraged and in the midst of some type of great difficulty—God, through the book of James, gives you practical ways to live out your faith. He shows you that He, indeed, has an app for every worldly problem and spiritual need you may face.

It is interesting to note that the word "application" is defined as "the act of putting to a special use or purpose."[15] Furthermore, Wikipedia explains that our modern-day "apps" are designed to "help solve problems in the real world."[16] When you download *God's* apps, you are putting to special purpose the truths from His Word, which will help solve your problems in the real world! It's so simple and guaranteed that you will wonder why you didn't utilize these supernatural apps sooner.

It is my prayer that you will fall in love with the Bible, which has the answers to all your questions and the power to renew your heart and mind (see Rom. 12:2) and provide long-lasting victory over the challenges of life. I pray that your faith will be strengthened as you find practical answers to the issues that have been distressing you for years. And if you ever find yourself lying awake contemplating life's perplexities, may you quickly and easily fall back to sleep, resting in the knowledge that your heavenly Father always has an app for all your needs, both great and small.

God Has an App to
# Turn Stress into Joy

## James 1:1-12

Have you ever thought about the people who lived in biblical times and surmised that they had it pretty easy? I have. While I thoroughly appreciate such modern conveniences as refrigeration, electricity, medicine, drive-thru Mexican food, cell phones, cars, airplanes, the Internet and watching college football on a high-definition television, I sometimes wonder if my life would be a lot simpler and a lot less stressful if these amenities didn't exist. On any given day, an abundance of voicemail and text messages press me for response, in addition to a long list of lingering emails in my inbox. There are meetings to attend, appointments to keep, quality time to spend with family, "honey-do"s around the house, a church to lead with 21 different worship services in various venues each weekend, books and blogs to write, employees to encourage . . . and the list goes on.

*Wouldn't it have been easier if I had lived during the time of the first-century church?* I ponder. After all, what kinds of things did people in that day worry about? Whether the thatched roof needed repairing? Who stole Larry's prized chicken? Whether or not the outdoor market would be closed due to rain? They didn't worry about managing social media accounts or answering phone calls. They had no vehicles or appliances to repair; no long work commutes or exorbitant gas prices to pay. Theirs was a life free from cares and concerns, right?

If you're starting to imagine biblical times as a peaceful life of eating falafel on the front porch of your stone house, let me explain a few things. In the introduction to his first chapter, the New Testament writer James identifies his readers as "the twelve tribes scattered among the nations" (Jas. 1:1). They were the Jewish Christians who were dispersed throughout the Mediterranean world. They were descendants of the 12 tribes of Jacob, the nation of Israel, who had come to believe that Jesus was the Christ, the long-awaited Messiah. And though they came from many different tribes, backgrounds and languages, James knew they had one thing in common: They were suffering.

You see, first-century Jewish believers faced much persecution because of their faith. Some lost their jobs and their families, while others were thrown into prison or even martyred for their faith.[1] I'm sure that some of them were thinking, *Why have I had nothing but problems plague my life since I became a Christian?* (Do you ever feel that way?)

On top of that, conflict had entered the Church, and some Christians had fallen back into some old habits that were not honoring to the Lord.[2] Vacillating between their faith and a worldly lifestyle, these new believers were failing to put their faith into practice, apply the Word of God, or show love and compassion toward one another (see Jas. 1–2). Perhaps James received reports of their struggles or heard murmurings of their backsliding. By whatever means the news reached his ears, James responded by writing a letter that is chock-full of spiritual guidance and hope, which these early Christians so desperately needed. While James offered this encouragement more than two millennia ago, it's still incredibly applicable to your life and mine.

## The Inevitability of Trials

Benjamin Franklin once said there are two things of which we can be certain: *death* and *taxes*.[3] With all due respect to one of our country's dear forefathers, I would like to add *stress* to the list—and I'm certain James would agree with me as I look at the language of his letter to believers: "Consider it pure joy, my brothers, whenever you face *trials* of many kinds" (Jas. 1:2, emphasis added).

Stress and trials are interrelated. A trial is the act of trying or testing,[4] while stress—which is synonymous with anxiety, pressure, burden, worry or strain[5]—can be the result of a trial. Both stress and trials weigh us down, cause our hearts to beat faster, deprive us of sleep, magnify our worries and become the focus of our attention. Both prevent us from enjoying life to the fullest.

Notice that James 1:2 doesn't read, "*If* you face trials." It very pointedly pronounces, "*Whenever* you face trials," and not just a few trials, but "trials of *many kinds*"! I really like the way Peter puts it in 1 Peter 4:12: "Dear friends, do not be surprised at the painful trial you are suffering, as though something strange were happening to you." In other words, we shouldn't act like something weird or crazy is happening to us when we encounter difficulties—they're inevitable!

In a sinful world, everyone most assuredly will encounter many forms of trials and stress, and believers are no exception. Yet this is often a great misconception in the minds of new believers—the idea that salvation earns us a "Get Out of Pain Free" pass similar to the "Get Out of Jail Free" card in the game of Monopoly. This simply is not true. Life is not a game, and stresses of every kind will undoubtedly rise against us when we least expect it.

Several Scriptures in addition to this passage in James echo this reality. King David wrote, "A righteous man may have many troubles" (Ps. 34:19). Even our Lord warned us that hardships are inevitable: "In this world you will have trouble" (John 16:33).

In the past few years, the American Psychological Association has published a report called "Stress in America," which tracks the stress levels, demographics, causes and impact of stress in the nation.[6] The most recent study released shows that in Los Angeles, where I live, stress levels are higher than the national average.[7] I almost laughed out loud when I read this, because I didn't need a report to give me that tidbit of information. And I'm sure that wherever you live, you would consider *it* to be the most stressful place—and for you, that's all that really matters! The fact is, just about every person in America is "living with moderate or high levels of stress, and while they understand this is not healthy, they're stymied in their efforts to make changes."[8]

Stress has been around since the beginning of creation, when Adam and Eve sinned in the Garden of Eden and, out of guilt and shame, made a futile attempt to hide from God (see Gen. 3). In the next chapter of the Bible (Gen. 4), lying, jealousy and murder emerged, irreversibly marring our earthly experience. I can imagine how Eve, the first mother in human history, mourned over the body of her slaughtered son Abel, who was killed by his own brother, Cain. Pain was part of the human experience then, and it is equally present now.

Today our lives are swamped with all kinds of suffering, temptation and trouble. Simply turning on the television to your local news station or flipping through the daily newspaper reveals that we are surrounded by all manner of terrible events and evils that bring deep heartache, emotional wounds and physical harm.

We're going to download an app to deal with these issues, but first, let's take a quick look at several of the most common causes of stress. Which of these have you experienced?

### So Much to Do, So Little Time

What does your to-do list look like on any given day? Maybe you make a quick stop at Starbucks to grab a coffee, the other "breakfast of champions," before an 8:00 A.M. conference call. Then it's meetings through the afternoon and a 30-minute workout at the gym. You may have to pick up your children from school and whisk them to soccer practice or piano lessons or a swim meet. Next, you hurry home to cook dinner by 6:30 P.M. while perusing Facebook and trying to help with homework.

Just as you get the kids tucked into bed, you remember that you're supposed to call Sheila to discuss next week's carpool schedule. You may be able to shoehorn your favorite show at 9:00 P.M., finish the proposal for your boss by 11:00 P.M. and then book your family's flights online for the vacation that seems light years away. Finally, you shuffle off to bed, completely spent and overwhelmed by the reality that it all starts again tomorrow.

Two thousand years ago, Martha mastered the art of maintaining a teeming to-do list. As her sister, Mary, sat on the floor near Jesus' feet, utterly captivated by His teachings, Martha scurried by, carrying heavy plates to the table. She wanted supper to be just perfect for their guests. Back in the kitchen area, she prepared the bread and poured olive oil into a dish, all the while casting sharp glances at her oblivious sister. *Mary's staring at Jesus like a three-year-old during story time,* she thought. *The Messiah is here in our home, and she's just sitting there instead of helping me serve Him and the disciples.*

Grabbing the tray of bread and oil, she stormed over to Jesus' side and said, "Lord, don't you care that my sister has left me to do the work by myself? Tell her to help me!" "Martha, Martha," Jesus answered, "you are worried and upset about many things, but few things are needed—or indeed only one. Mary has chosen what is better, and it will not be taken away from her" (Luke 10:40-42).

Time with God and with family is our greatest and most precious commodity, and yet we busily power through life. Will Rogers, the famous actor, comedian and social commentator of the 1920s and '30s, once observed, "Half our life is spent trying to find something to do with the time we have rushed through life trying to save."[9] In the end, when all of our rushing stops and our to-do lists are complete, it will seem like the entirety of our existence was no more than a blip on the radar screen of life.

## Unavoidable Loss

My friend Tom staggered into my office, sinking into the cushy chair across from me. It was 10 days before his much-anticipated wedding, but seeing his dejected expression clued me in that something was terribly wrong. Tom explained that he had just received an earth-shattering phone call. His father, who was without question his best friend, had just committed suicide.

When approximately 150,000 people in the world die every single day,[10] it doesn't take long before each of us, without exception, is confronted with the seemingly cruel and untimely death of a loved one. Then, with a deeply wounded heart, and in the midst of our mourning, we are thrust into the inevitable position of having to make funeral arrangements. We answer a hundred questions in a funeral home about the casket, flowers, program and invitees, which only add stress to an already difficult situation.

The death of a loved one isn't the only type of devastating loss, for a relationship, a career or a treasured possession can be taken from us in a moment's time. We can lose a special talent or ability—reflect on a painter who loses his eyesight, a singer who loses her voice, an athlete who sustains an injury that ends his promising career. For these individuals, life is forever altered.

Job was a man who experienced firsthand the stress caused by loss. It all started when a messenger burst through the door of his house, sweating profusely and barely able to catch his breath, and said, "Sir, the Sabeans attacked and carried away all the oxen and donkeys. They killed all your servants, and I'm the only one who has escaped to tell you!"

While this man was still speaking, the Bible says that another messenger arrived and exclaimed, "Job! A strange fire fell from the sky and burned up the sheep and the servants, and I'm the only one who has escaped to tell you!" And while that servant was still speaking, another man entered the house and explained that the Chaldeans had carried off all of Job's camels and killed the other servants.

Before that messenger could finish his eyewitness testimony, yet another servant arrived, trembling and clutching his cap. He swallowed hard. "Sir," he stammered, "your sons and daughters were feasting and drinking at your eldest son's house, when suddenly a mighty wind swept in from the desert and struck the house. It collapsed on them . . . and they are all dead" (see Job 1:13-19).

As if losing all 10 of his children wasn't heart-wrenching enough, we read later, in Job 2:7, that Satan afflicted Job with painful sores from the soles of his feet to the top of his head. This poor man's life was in total shambles. From his livestock, to his servants, to his children, and finally, to his health, he had lost absolutely everything.

Job's tragic story exemplifies the fact that nothing in life is lasting; loss is unavoidable and leads to much stress upon the heart and spirit.

## Lack of Provision

Many of us have known, at one time or another, what it's like to struggle for our basic needs. Are you a student trying to determine how you will afford next semester's tuition? Are you, like so many others in this country, unemployed, deluged by unpaid bills and under tremendous pressure to find work so you can provide for your family? Has your final attempt to save your home been denied and you're about to undergo foreclosure? Maybe you don't have the funds to repair your vehicle so that you can get from point A to point B. Or perhaps you are lonely and have been praying, longing and waiting for a companion. Whatever your situation, know that you are not alone in your need of provision.

Consider the moving story in 1 Kings 17 about a widow left to raise her son alone during a time of severe famine. God commanded the prophet Elijah to go to this woman in the small Phoenician town of Zarephath. So he went there and found the widow gathering sticks by the town gate. He called to her and said, "Would you bring me a little water in a jar so I may have a drink? . . . And bring me, please, a piece of bread." The woman replied, "As surely as the LORD your God lives . . . I don't have any bread—only a handful of flour in a jar and a little oil in a jug. I am gathering a few sticks to take home and make a meal for myself and my son, that we may eat it—and die" (1 Kings 17:10-12).

Can you fathom the deplorable state of this poor woman? After losing her husband, she was unable to provide for her and her beloved boy's basic needs. Imagine her in the kitchen, wiping salty tears from her eyes as she scrounges for scraps of food. She musters a feeble smile and prays that her son won't see her despair; she knows that these scraps will be their last few bites of food before starvation calls them to an early grave. The Zarephath widow knew what it was to be desperate for provision. Being unable to provide the bare essentials for one's family is quite possibly life's biggest stress.

### Degrees of Oppression and Ridicule

Any time you decide to stand for God at home, work or school—especially in our culture that is becoming more and more opposed to the Bible—you are going to face pressure, stress and different forms of persecution (see 2 Tim. 3:12). Daniel encountered this truth up close and personally, for he was a man of great faith and conviction.

Of the 120 governors that Darius, the king of Persia, had appointed to rule over his various provinces, Daniel was the cream of the crop. But his success led the other administrators to become very jealous of him, and they knew that the only way to bring him to ruin was to make his faith illegal. With the worst of intentions, they convinced King Darius to enforce an irreversible law stating that anyone who prayed to any god or man besides the king during the next 30 days would be thrown into the lions' den.

When Daniel learned of this dreadful news, he returned home to his upstairs room where the windows opened toward Jerusalem. He knelt down on the floor three times a day, praying and giving thanks to his God as he had always done. Of course, Daniel's enemies soon caught him in the act and alerted the king.

Darius was greatly distressed and made every effort to rescue Daniel, but the administrators reminded the king that the edict could not be changed or repealed. Daniel 6:16 records what happened next: "So the king gave the order, and they brought Daniel and threw him into the lions' den. The king said to Daniel, 'May your God, whom you serve continually, rescue you!'" A stone was brought and placed over the mouth of the den, and the king sealed it with his own signet ring and with the rings of his nobles, so that Daniel's situation might not be changed.

Like Daniel, if you've ever faced persecution—whether it be at school, among family and friends, or in the workplace—you are familiar with the lump in your throat, a racing heart, sweating palms and the uncertainty of how the situation will turn out. In the last century alone, more Christians have been martyred for their faith in God than in all the previous centuries combined.[11] From taunting and ostracism in one's social circles, to oppression and death under anti-Christian governments, we will most assuredly encounter stress as a result of the glorious name we lift up.

Our common experiences with overwhelming to-do lists, unavoidable losses, lack of provision and varying degrees of oppression and ridicule show us how true James's words are that we will indeed face trials of many kinds! In fact, the precursor to downloading God's app for those who are stressed is to *understand and acknowledge that trials are simply an inevitable part of life*. With that understanding, you can begin to download God's app to turn stress into joy!

For the rest of this chapter, let's look at six steps that comprise the "download" of your joy app and focus on scriptural ways to keep life's unavoidable stresses at bay.

**BEGIN DOWNLOAD**

0%     10%     20%     30%     40%     50%     60%     70%     80%     90%

## Step 1: Consider the Blessings Among the Briars

Anxiety pressed down on the pit of my stomach during what was supposed to be one of the most thrilling days of my life. After all, how often does a person get invited to the most important basketball game of the year? Yet, there I was, sitting in the passenger seat as my friend, Patrick Bet-David, drove down the Los Angeles 210 Freeway in bumper-to-bumper traffic. I was trying to listen as he enthusiastically spoke about the success of his business and the future plans of his family, but I must admit that I was a bit distracted. I couldn't stop thinking about the extraordinary sporting event between the Los Angeles Lakers and the Boston Celtics that we were about to attend.

I was thankful we had left early enough so that we would have no problem making it to the game on time. All of a sudden, something strange happened. It appeared as though all the other vehicles began to pick up speed and pass us by; but it turned out that we were the ones slowing down. Drivers swerved around and past us, honking their horns and calling us names that a pastor should not repeat.

"Oh no," Patrick said. "I think I'm out of gas."

"What do you mean you're out of gas?" I asked.

"I knew I was running low," he said, "but it never means empty when it says empty."

With hazard lights on, he coasted over to the side of the freeway, parked the car and dialed roadside assistance on his cell phone. I was in total shock, but I did my best to keep my cool. Meanwhile, some 45 minutes later, we were still waiting for the auto service truck to show up.

My family and friends would easily understand my frustration at that moment. It's no secret to them that I have both coached and played basketball for many years, and I absolutely love the Los Angeles Lakers. So when Patrick invited me to Game 7 of the 2010 NBA Championship Finals, I couldn't believe it! It was a dream come true.

As we both stepped out of the car and stood among the weeds and briars along the 210 freeway in the June heat of Southern California, I was starting to feel as if I were in a nightmare. *This can't be happening,* I thought. *We've missed the opening ceremony, and there goes the start of the first quarter. Who runs out of gas anyway?* I found myself looking for a hidden camera just to make sure I wasn't being *Punk'd.*

Then Patrick turned to me and said something I will never forget: "Smile, Dudley! People would give anything to be in our situation!"

"What in the world are you talking about?" I asked. "I'm supposed to be at the Staples Center, cheering for the Lakers, but instead I'm picking thorns out of my socks on the side of this smog-filled freeway."

"Hey, we live in the greatest city in the world, and we're blessed to be alive!" he replied exuberantly. "We have roadside service on its way to bring us gas, and in a few moments, we'll be at Game 7 of the NBA Finals. There are millions of people who would count themselves blessed to be in our shoes right now."

Ever the optimist, my friend was right. I needed an attitude adjustment. This was a momentary bump in the road, help was on the way, and we were truly blessed. (Visit www.GodHasAnApp.com to see a video of us with roadside assistance.)

In the midst of stressful situations, we find this encouragement in James 1:2: "Consider it pure joy, my brothers and sisters, whenever you face trials of many kinds." Though this may seem counterintuitive—such as when Jesus told us to love our enemy, forgive our brother and turn the other cheek—it is critical to our app download. When we are stressed, lonely, jobless, brokenhearted or facing poor health, we are to consider it pure joy.

Now, before you jump to the conclusion that James is out of his mind, let's determine what he means by the word "consider." He absolutely is not asking us to ignore our stress. Nor does he take us for fools, suggesting that we think trials are actually pleasant. Friend, please know that being a Christian does not require you to pretend that everything is all right when it isn't. But if you look more closely at James's choice of words, he is prompting you to simply ponder carefully or change your outlook about trials, and you'll understand why you need this new perspective throughout the course of this download.

Second, let's uncover what the word "joy" means in James's seemingly absurd suggestion. To consider trials as pure joy does not mean to be giddy or excited when you're experiencing stress. It does not mean that you should be laughing instead of crying, or celebrating instead of mourning. James is not referring to an external emotional response, but rather to an internal disposition of true peace, regardless of the circumstances. Romans 8:28 says that in all things—whether pleasant or painful—the Lord is working for the good of those who love Him and are called according to His purpose. Therefore, you can rest your head on your pillow each night, knowing beyond a doubt that God has everything under control. This is what James means by "pure joy."

As we stood on the side of the busy, thorny 210 freeway, my friend was so kind to remind me that finding joy in the midst of stress is all about considering the blessings among the briars. You and I can do this by taking a step back from our momentary troubles to thank God for His goodness and appreciate what's important in life. If you're not already doing so, make it a habit to thank Him at the beginning, middle and end of each day. And when you're feeling completely stressed out, pause for a moment and ponder the list of good things in your life, however short that list may be. Are you healthy? Do you have a job? Do you have food to eat and clean water to drink? Do you have at least one person in your life who loves you? Do you serve a God who cares for you and has everything under control? Good! Thank God for those things!

When your heart is focused on the blessings among the briars, you realize that everything you thought was important—like missing the opening of Game 7 of the NBA Finals—really is of no consequence in the grand scheme of God's perfect plan for your life. When gratitude becomes your goal, something amazing happens: The stress that felt like an irritating thorn in your sock suddenly disappears . . . and it is replaced by indescribable joy.

**DOWNLOAD IN PROGRESS**

■■■■■■■■■■■□□□□□□□□□□□□□□□□□□□□□□□□□□□□□□□□□□■

0%      10%     20%     30%     40%     50%     60%     70%     80%     90%

## Step 2: Understand that Perseverance Makes Perfect

As we continue reading James 1:3, our author divulges *why* we can consider stress and trials pure joy: "Because you know that the testing of your faith produces perseverance." The word "testing" comes from the Greek word *dokimion*, an adjective that means "genuine" or "without alloy."[12] Thus, the noun form we see in the text means, quite literally, a "test to prove genuine."

Nineteenth-century Christian theologian and author Søren Kierkegaard once wrote, "Adversities do not make a person weak, they reveal what strength he has." Like a young cadet in military boot camp, your endurance and commitment are being tested as you are made stronger. You continually press forward to see what you are capable of; and though the process may be painful, your perseverance in the face of "trials of many kinds" unveils your faith as genuine.

Moreover, you can endure the season of testing, knowing there is an end in sight. When you took a test in school, there was a start and a finish. There was a moment when the instructor said, "All right, students, time is up. Please put your pencils down." Likewise, you have to ride the bumps of life with steadfast resolve, knowing that the bumps (the testing) will come to a conclusion at some point.

On a recent flight from Indianapolis to Los Angeles, the plane on which I was traveling encountered severe turbulence. I fly frequently and have experienced several turbulent flights, but this by far was one of the worst. When my coffee started splashing around and spilling out of the cup, I thought, *Well, this can't be good.*

Finally, the pilot's voice interrupted the trepidation that all of us passengers undoubtedly were feeling. "Hello, folks," he said. "Obviously, we've hit some rough turbulence. We've tried many different altitudes and, believe or not, this is the best one. The bad news is that we've got about 100 miles of this to travel through." As soon as the captain said this, you could hear a collective groan from the passengers. But then he continued, "The good news is that we're traveling at 8 miles a minute, so it's only going to take a little more than 10 minutes to get through it."

That announcement put things in perspective! I realized the present stress was simply a part of the process we passengers had to go through to get from point A to point B—and I felt a whole lot better knowing that the turbulence wasn't going to last forever. If you are in the worst storm of your life right now, and you don't think you will ever get through it, know this: *You are not going to remain in the storm forever; and your persistence through it is making you a better person.* Your job and mine is to patiently persevere through times of testing.

According to James 1:4, not only is perseverance the purpose of our testing, but there is also a purpose to perseverance: "Let perseverance finish its work so that you may be mature and complete, not lacking anything." Are you low on patience? Do you wrestle with pride? Are you easily angered? Are you constantly anxious or afraid? Without a doubt, all of us struggle with issues that hinder our spiritual completion. But in order to develop the godly virtues of patience, humility, grace, peace, trust and courage—to mature spiritually—we must persevere in our struggle with stress.

Faith that perseveres is the highest quality of faith. Holding on to this truth allows us to run our spiritual race as men and women who have been conditioned to press on. But it doesn't end there!

The *New King James Version* translates James 1:4 this way: "But let patience have its perfect work, that you may be *perfect* and complete, lacking nothing" (emphasis added). Like a clump of clay on a potter's wheel, God is smoothing the lumps and rough edges until you become a flawless vessel to be used for His glory. When you know that God is molding and shaping you, you actually end up loving (or at least appreciating) the process!

Our God, the creator of the universe, cares about you enough to spend His time working on your spiritual improvement and completion through the stresses you encounter. Just as gold could not be made pure without high temperature heating or chemical exposure, our spiritual maturity would not be possible without the presence of trials. Moreover, you can have joy in knowing that everything you go through prepares you for the work the Lord wants you to do in the future. You will become a better husband or wife, boss or employee, brother or sister, son or daughter, friend and servant of God. You need not succumb to fear or intimidation, nor run away from stress or hardships, because our heavenly Father will give you the utmost confidence in every situation. And that is reason to rejoice!

**DOWNLOAD IN PROGRESS**

0%    10%    20%    30%    40%    50%    60%    70%    80%    90%

## Step 3: Wise Up

The world was at King Solomon's fingertips. He had just formed a powerful alliance with Egypt by marrying Pharaoh's daughter (see 1 Kings 3:1), and he carried on the blessed legacy of his father David as he ruled the nation of Israel. One night, God appeared to

Solomon in a dream and said, "Ask for whatever you want me to give you" (1 Kings 3:5).

Can you imagine being presented with such an opportunity? What would you ask for? The old tales of a magic genie granting three wishes come to mind—along with the men in these stories requesting boundless wealth, power, fame, immortality and beautiful women. Solomon could have asked for any of these things, but he didn't. Here is the king's humble and sincere response:

> Your servant is here among the people you have chosen, a great people, too numerous to count or number. So give your servant a discerning heart to govern your people and to distinguish between right and wrong. For who is able to govern this great people of yours? (vv. 8-9).

The Word says that God was very pleased with Solomon's request and replied:

> Since you have asked for this and not for long life or wealth for yourself, nor have asked for the death of your enemies but for discernment in administering justice, I will do what you have asked. I will give you a wise and discerning heart, so that there will never have been anyone like you, nor will there ever be. Moreover, I will give you what you have not asked for—both wealth and honor—so that in your lifetime you will have no equal among kings. And if you walk in obedience to me and keep my decrees and commands as David your father did, I will give you a long life (1 Kings 3:11-15).

I can imagine that as King Solomon oversaw a people "too numerous to count," each coming to him with problems and issues, and desiring his earnest judgment, he must have experienced a level of stress that you and I have never had to face. Then he is given the unique chance to ask anything from God. If I had to juggle all of the responsibilities of this exceptional king, I might have asked for a vacation! However, that is not what Solomon chose. Though he could have had the gold of Egypt or the oil of Babylon, he asked God for wisdom, above all other things. Thus, God gave it to him, and so much more.

Thinking back to our story about Martha and Mary, you'll recall that Mary also chose wisdom. This seemingly sedentary sister seized the once-in-a-lifetime opportunity to sit at the feet of the Savior of the world and hear firsthand the words that would alter the course of history. Martha, on the other hand, needed Jesus to remind her gently to give up her worries and choose what is better.

This very God who gave Solomon wisdom and spoke life-changing words to Martha and Mary is willing to give you wisdom as well. All you have to do is ask. In the middle of stressful times, notice what James 1:5 asserts: "If any of you lacks wisdom, you should ask God, who gives generously to all without finding fault, and it will be given to you."

Solomon knew that if he had wisdom, he would have everything else. If you and I follow this extraordinary king's example by asking God for a wise and discerning heart, we will quickly see our stresses transformed into joy. That is because wisdom is of chief importance when we tackle life's greatest challenges.

You can glean wisdom by looking up—to God—as Solomon did, seeking Him with your whole heart, soul and strength (see Deut. 6:5). Then, simply ask Him for a wise and discerning heart. James says that when you ask God for wisdom, He "gives generously to all without finding fault" (Jas. 1:5). That's a promise you can take to the bank as you exchange your stress for pure joy!

**DOWNLOAD IN PROGRESS**

0%   10%   20%   30%   40%   50%   60%   70%   80%   90%

## Step 4: Put Down the Ping-Pong Paddle

When asking God for wisdom as you deal with various stresses, James delivers an important caveat: "But when you ask, you must believe and not doubt, because the one who doubts is like a wave of the sea, blown and tossed by the wind" (Jas. 1:6). How familiar to you is the following scenario? You are worried and stressed about work, about your children, your finances or the health of a family member. Your mind is constantly preoccupied with stressful thoughts, and you lose sleep each night. All of a sudden, it occurs to you to ask God to help you, to work out your circumstances and show you what to do, and you feel a sense of peace and wisdom settle into your heart like the warmth of a perfect spring day. But just as quickly as ominous clouds move across the sky and pour buckets of rain on an afternoon picnic, the worries return and you feel hopeless and stressed out once again.

This is spiritual Ping-Pong, my friend. To trust God one moment and to return to a place of fretting and fussing the next is equivalent to going back and forth like "a wave of the sea, blown and tossed by the wind," as James so aptly puts it. What's more, one who is engaged in this futile game of Ping-Pong "should not expect to receive anything from the Lord" (Jas. 1:7), for this sort of wavering is not pleasing to Him. "Such a person is double-minded and unstable in all they do" (v. 8).

How do we put down the Ping-Pong paddle in order to turn our stress into joy? Our minds can be terribly fickle, but the apostle Paul challenges us to practice the skill of taking "captive every thought to make it obedient to Christ" (2 Cor. 10:5). Furthermore, he gives us more practical insight in Philippians 4:6-7: "Do not be anxious about anything, but in every situation, by prayer and petition, with thanksgiving, present your requests to God. And the peace of God, which transcends all understanding, will guard your hearts and your minds in Christ Jesus."

Not only will prayer and petition (asking God) alleviate our anxieties and help us experience peace during times of stress, but Paul gives us one more critical step: "Whatever is true, whatever is noble, whatever is right, whatever is pure, whatever is lovely, whatever is admirable—if anything is excellent or praiseworthy—think about such things" (Phil. 4:8). Whenever you are tempted to let worries dominate your thoughts, immediately set your mind upon that which is good. For me, there is nothing more true, noble, right, pure, lovely, admirable, excellent or praise-worthy than the Word of God, so I use these times to memorize and meditate on encouraging Scriptures.

One passage of Scripture you can always return to for encour-agement is Daniel 6, for it is an excellent example of the type of unwavering faith that God honors. Even in the face of death, Daniel didn't forsake his trust in the Lord. I am convinced that as the ferocious beasts encircled him—their guttural growls causing the hair on the back of his neck to stand—Daniel remained un-afraid. After all, this is the same man who prayed to God three times a day in spite of a royal edict forbidding such faithful devo-tion. But let's examine verses 19-22 for further proof of Daniel's steadfast courage:

> At the first light of dawn, the king got up and hurried to the lions' den. When he came near the den, he called to Daniel in an anguished voice, "Daniel, servant of the living God, has your God, whom you serve continually, been able to rescue you from the lions?" Daniel answered, "May the king live forever! My God sent his angel, and he shut the mouths of the lions. They have not hurt me, because I was found innocent in his sight."

How would you have reacted if you were standing in that dark, dank lions' den and you realized that God literally had shut the mouths of these fierce creatures so they couldn't harm you? If it were me, I'd probably be tempted to reach out and pet one of them—maybe take another one for a ride! I would be *overjoyed* that God had saved me from persecution and death.

So, whenever stress is closing in on you, ponder this amazing story, and I guarantee it will bring your heart joy to recall how God rescued Daniel from not only his persecutors but also from the mouths of hungry lions. Daniel refused to play spiritual Ping-Pong, and his faith and commitment to the Lord remained un-shakable. When you do the same, God can and will deliver you from your most intimidating adversary.

**DOWNLOAD IN PROGRESS**

0%    10%    20%    30%    40%    50%    60%    70%    80%    90%

## Step 5: Take Pride in Humility

The poor widow from Zarephath, whose story is recorded in 1 Kings 17, had become well acquainted with the ache in her lower back resulting from her lowly posture while gathering sticks of wood at the town gate and spending countless hours in prayer as she begged God for a miracle. She had poured out everything she had—her grief over her deceased husband, her strength in caring for her young son, her efforts in trying to find work to provide food for the two of them—and now a new visitor in town required just a little more. But that little bit would surely wring her out completely.

"Don't be afraid," Elijah said to her. "Go home and do as you have said. But first make a small loaf of bread for me from what you have and bring it to me, and then make something for yourself and your son" (1 Kings 17:13).

As kind and giving as this dear woman may have been, she had to have been thinking, *Lord, I know how much flour and oil are left in my bare cupboard. After I make this man a small cake of bread there won't be anything left for my son and me. I've given all I have, and now the tiny scrap of food I have left I must give away.*

With an intimate knowledge of the power and provision of God, Elijah declared, "This is what the LORD, the God of Israel, says: 'The jar of flour will not be used up and the jug of oil will not run dry until the day the LORD sends rain on the land'" (v. 14).

So the widow went home and did what Elijah had instructed her to do. Here's what the Bible says happened next: "There was food every day for Elijah and for the woman and her family. For the jar of flour was not used up and the jug of oil did not run dry, in keeping with the word of the LORD spoken by Elijah" (vv. 15-16).

Because of the widow's humility, her willingness to put the needs of a stranger above her own and her trust in God's provision, she was able to be a part of something truly miraculous. James 1:9 exhorts, "Believers in humble circumstances ought to take pride in their high position." This is the opposite of what we tend to do, isn't it? When times get tough, our trust in God's provision fades and we want to take the bull by the horns and fix things. In reality, there are many times when victory only comes when we let go—when we fully and humbly rely on God.

Over and over again, the Bible reiterates the anthem of God's tender regard for those who are humble (see Pss. 147:6; 149:4; Prov. 3:34). Psalm 149:4 tells us that the Lord crowns the humble with victory; and He declares in Isaiah 66:2, "These are the ones I look on with favor: those who are humble and contrite in spirit, and who tremble at my word." The more we are emptied of pride and self, the more room we have for the power of God to move in and work in our lives!

Jesus of Nazareth was the epitome of humility, and we are to emulate His humble spirit, love, tenderness, and compassion— not looking out for our own interests, but for the interests of others (see Phil. 2:1-5). This passage in Philippians 2:6-11 explains that Jesus, "being in very nature God, did not consider equality with God something to be used to his own advantage; rather, he made himself nothing by taking the very nature of a servant, being made in human likeness. And being found in appearance as a man, he humbled himself by becoming obedient to death—even death on a cross!"

Our Lord knew that nothing was more valuable than the posture of a humble servant, and He did not succumb to the lure of power, prestige or temporary riches, the longevity of which James 1:10-11 compares to a wildflower. Sure, the flower looks attractive and vibrant. But with the scorching heat of a single afternoon, the once beautiful blossom withers and is no more.

When we understand the fleeting nature of our world and everything in it, we are compelled to disregard that which we tend to cling to—power, position and prosperity. Consider this: Doesn't most of our stress here on earth stem from a fear of losing something we can't hold on to anyway? But if we can take pride in humility as instructed by God's Word, the things of this world grow strangely dim.

No matter what provision may be running low in your life and causing you stress, be patient and trust in the Lord. Like the widow's small measure of flour and oil that kept miraculously replenishing, rest in the fact that you serve a God who has limitless resources at His fingertips. Instead of trusting in yourself, trust in the One who has the ability to lift you up in due time. As Jesus Christ said, "Those who exalt themselves will be humbled, and those who humble themselves will be exalted" (Matt. 23:12).

## Step 6: Have Faith in "the Latter"

The early part of Glenn Cunningham's life was marked by considerable tragedy. Born in Elkhart, Kansas, Glenn survived a furious schoolhouse fire that claimed the life of his 10-year-old brother, Floyd, and badly burned Glenn's legs. He lost all the flesh on his knees and shins, all the toes on his left foot, and his transverse arch was nearly destroyed. The doctors recommended amputating Glenn's legs, but this so distressed young Glenn that his parents wouldn't allow it.[13]

"All right," the experts said, "but your boy will probably never walk normally again."

And yet, with fierce determination, Glenn gradually regained his mobility. He began by following a plow across the fields, leaning on it for support, and then he engaged in tireless experimentation to see what he could do with his legs.[14] Because of his persistence, the latter part of Glenn's life was highlighted by great victory. Considered by many to be the greatest American miler of all time, and nicknamed the "Kansas Flyer" and the "Elkhart Express," Glenn Cunningham was a distance runner who set the world record for the mile run in 1934. At the 1936 Olympics, he won the silver medal in the 1500-meter race.

Praise be to God that Glenn did not give up when he was a boy, for the physical, mental and emotional stress he endured surely fueled his faith, his passion and his indomitable spirit to achieve the impossible. His testimony serves as a reminder that we are promised a greater reward in "the latter." Take a look at the assurance we find in James 1:12: "Blessed is the one who perseveres under trial because, having stood the test, that person will receive the crown of life that the Lord has promised to those who love him."

Sometimes this blessing occurs while we are still alive here on earth, as in Job's case. After a seemingly endless assailment of grief and tribulation, Job never wavered in his love and reverence for the Lord. We read these final words in Job 42:12-13,16-17:

> The LORD blessed the *latter part* of Job's life more than the first. He had fourteen thousand sheep, six thousand camels, a thousand yoke of oxen and a thousand donkeys. And he also had seven sons and three daughters. . . . After this, Job lived a hundred and forty years; he saw his children and their children to the fourth generation. And so Job died, an old man and full of years (emphasis added).

While your future blessing in this life may not be as abundant as Job's—sometimes our reward is not received until heaven (see Matt. 5:12 and 16:27)—his story is an encouragement to persevere in stressful or difficult seasons, having faith in the latter. This is an integral part of God's app to turn stress into joy. *Today* you and I can rejoice in knowing that God is working on our behalf and that restoration is right around the corner.

It reminds me of an episode of *Overhaulin'* I watched recently on TV; it's a show on TLC (The Learning Channel) in which they take an old beat-up car and give it an extreme makeover, to the joyful surprise of the car's owner. In this particular installment, a woman in Los Angeles had been notified that her car had been impounded. What had actually happened is that the producers of the *Overhaulin'* show had stealthily taken her car for the purpose of fixing it up and returning it to her in mint condition. The woman didn't know this, of course, so she called the fake impound number, which was really the *Overhaulin'* team, and demanded to know where her car was.

To buy some time for the makeover, they told her they had mistakenly sent it down to San Diego and asked her to call back the next day. When she did, they told her sheepishly, "Ma'am, you're not going to believe this, but your car was sent to Orange County this time. You're going to have to come down and pick it up."

The woman was livid. She cursed them out and yelled and screamed, and didn't want to go to Orange County. Unbeknownst to her, people were working diligently to improve her situation by restoring her car beyond her wildest dreams. But she couldn't see that. She could only see her present situation, which is the only thing a lot of us see. When we undergo relentless stress, we curse God; we complain and kick and scream. We can't see what He's doing. However, you and I must trust in the Lord, knowing that in the midst of loss or stress, He's slowly but surely working behind the scenes on our behalf.

After the *Overhaulin'* team revealed the woman's completely refurbished car, she was astonished. She jumped up and down and praised them with tears in her eyes and a big smile on her face. Likewise, when God reveals to you what He has been doing in your heart, your life and your circumstances—*through* all the stressful circumstances—you, too, will jump for joy and praise His matchless name.

### DOWNLOAD COMPLETE!

| 0% | 10% | 20% | 30% | 40% | 50% | 60% | 70% | 80% | 90% |

Congratulations! You have officially downloaded God's app to turn stress into joy by acknowledging first and foremost that we *all* will face trials of many kinds, and by examining the four major causes of stress and diving into the Scriptures. More specifically, you have discovered six scriptural principles that will keep you focused on joy as you practice them whenever you are in the midst of a stressful circumstance:

- Consider the blessings among the briars.
- Understand that perseverance makes perfect.
- Determine that it is essential to ask God for wisdom.
- Put down the Ping-Pong paddle and refuse to vacillate between worry and trust in the Lord.
- Seek humility, and fully rely on God's providence.
- Resolve to have faith in the latter outcome of your stress or trial.

I close with the words of the apostle Peter, who was no stranger to stress. Like Paul, he faced much persecution in his life for the sake of the gospel of Jesus Christ. Church tradition holds that he was eventually martyred for his faith. And yet, his words, recorded in 1 Peter 1:6-8, reveal a stunning and firsthand perspective on extreme stress:

> In all this you greatly rejoice, though now for a little while you may have had to suffer grief in all kinds of trials. These have come so that the proven genuineness of your faith—of greater worth than gold, which perishes even though refined by fire—may result in praise, glory and honor when Jesus Christ is revealed. Though you have not seen him, you love him; and even though you do not see him now, you believe in him and are filled with an inexpressible and glorious joy.

Now that you have the app to turn stress into joy, what will you do with it? Dear friend, when you are stressed, you can choose to retreat, rebel or rejoice. My prayer is that you will *always* choose to rejoice (see Phil. 4:4).

God Has an App to

# Overcome Temptation

## James 1:13-27

In my opinion, one of the best burgers on the market is the Carl's Jr. Western Bacon Cheeseburger.[1] A masterpiece of fast-food cuisine, this burger boasts a hearty all-beef patty, two crispy slices of bacon, a blanket of melted American cheese, a sweet and tangy barbeque sauce and two thick onion rings. Some have accused it of being a heart attack served on a toasted bun.

Honestly, it isn't so much the calorie count that my conscience questions—it's the commercials. These television ads are noted for featuring scantily dressed young women consuming a burger while flaunting their feminine wiles. Essentially, Carl's Jr. uses sex to sell hamburgers.

Obviously, continuing to consume these burgers causes some guilt, because with every Western Bacon Cheeseburger I buy, I am encouraging Carl's Jr. to continue promoting their food with sexually provocative advertisements. And this dilemma causes me grief. Without question, I miss that tasty burger, but how could I buy another one knowing the company is going to continue to peddle their product in this manner?

Carl's Jr. isn't the only culprit. It is impossible to meander through the mall past certain stores without noticing their wall-length, racy advertisements of half-dressed young adults. Even a walk past the magazine rack at a bookstore, stocked with sensual images on the magazine covers, serves as a smorgasbord of visual temptation for even the most casual of readers.

No one can escape temptation in this culture. It's everywhere; it's no longer lurking in the shadows, but displayed proudly on billboards and in movie theaters, and even on our television and computer screens. We're constantly bombarded by images through a variety of media that appeal to the sensual appetite like never before.

It's slightly awkward to write about a topic like this. Frankly, it's kind of embarrassing to admit I struggle to live like Jesus or that, at any time in the day, I could be enticed to sin. No, not sin in necessarily an earth-shattering front-page news kind of way, but certainly in ways that would disappoint my Creator. I don't get a pass for being the pastor of a church, and I certainly don't get a pass for being a Christian. I'm tempted to sin just like everyone else.

However, there's a rumor circulating that is damaging to our Christian walk. It's the rumor that being tempted somehow makes you a bad person. I find this misconception baffling, but I've met with people who are devastated because their anger flared up or they considered lying or they entertained the idea of stealing. These conflicted individuals were absolutely disgusted with themselves. They wondered out loud, "What kind of person am I to even *consider* doing something wrong? After all, no one else has these desires, right?"

Let me squash this misconception right now. *Everyone is faced with temptation at some point or another.* Even those who wouldn't consider themselves "religious" recognize temptation when they see it. Our television sets are flooded with stories of people facing the temptations of power, drug abuse, overeating and lust. We tune in because we can relate. We like watching celebrities break drug addiction or the obese shed an amazingly significant number of pounds, because deep down, if these people could defeat a temptation so utterly consuming that it had controlled their lives, then maybe—just maybe—we too could break away from the parts of our lives that don't make us quite so proud. It gives us hope that maybe we could be better people.

The apostle Paul put it like this: "No temptation has seized you *except what is common to man*" (1 Cor. 10:13, emphasis added). In the Greek, "common to man" is one word.[2] If we wanted to translate Paul's words in another way, we could say, "No temptation has seized you except what is *human*." To be tempted is to be human. The fish of the sea and the birds of the air do not deal with temptation; they simply do what they must to survive. There is no higher law, no morality, for the animal world except to stay alive. Humans not only live under a much higher moral law, but we are also expected to follow that moral law to a tee.

So here's the deal: We are all tempted to sin. The difference between the Christian life and the worldly life is demonstrated by how we *respond* to temptation.

I'm always surprised when I see the severity of criticism leveled at celebrities caught in a misdeed. Even though the wrongdoing warrants some level of indignation, don't you get a little exhausted with the level of skepticism aimed at the likes of Lindsay Lohan or Charlie Sheen? And it's not just at actors or actresses or rock stars. Every time we see a news headline about another church pastor falling prey to the lures of pornography, or a professional athlete caught using steroids, or some politician involved in an extortion scheme, we shake our heads because another public figure has bitten the dust.

Yes, these personalities sometimes make monumental mistakes, but we're hardly exempt from similar temptations. For example, we all struggle with greed, regardless of the dollar amount. We have all been tempted in a myriad of ways, even if giving in to temptation won't land our pictures on the nightly news. More importantly, we've all given in to those temptations, even when God expects a different choice from us.

Every now and then, during a sermon or lesson on temptation, I'll ask the people sitting in the audience if they have ever stolen from someone, even if it was a couple of bucks from their father's dresser. Most of them will raise their hands as expected. Next, I'll ask if any of them have coveted their neighbors' possessions, such as an expensive car or a fancy television. Again, many of them will raise their hands. "Have any of you lied?" I'll ask, and at that question, I look for every hand in the room to shoot up—but without fail, there are always a few that do not. So I'll joke, "The person who didn't raise his or her hand is probably the biggest liar here!" After all, 1 John 1:10 says, "If we claim we have not sinned, we make him [Jesus] out to be a liar and his word has no place in our lives."

At the end of the day, every single one of us has given in to temptation. To yield to temptation is to travel through the "wide gate" of which Jesus spoke in Matthew 7:13, along the path that leads to severe consequences—even destruction. It's easy to take this path. It's well trodden and much travelled. The directional signs are clear, and the road is paved. A convenient moving sidewalk leading to the wide path is probably being installed even as I write! And there are plenty of companions along the way who encourage us to continue on the path leading to ruin. But they always forget to tell you about what lies ahead. They neglect to say that the last few yards of that pavement are marred with scorch marks and devastation.

The Christian walk follows a path through what Jesus calls "the narrow gate." It isn't decorated with rainbows and bunnies. Instead, it is littered with stumbling blocks and hazards. It is by no means an easy walk. At every turn a new temptation confronts us, threatening to knock us from the narrow path back to the paved wide road we know so well.

Temptation can be illustrated as a fishing lure. On the outside, it's colorful and shiny. Some lures have festive skirts; others have little whirligigs that spin around in the water. They come in all shapes, sizes and smells, but each one has the same purpose: to catch a fish. Beneath the decoration lies a hook waiting to snag some unsuspecting fish from the water, to their doom.

Temptation always seems innocent and enjoyable from the outside. That's what makes it tempting. But behind the vivid colors and the enticing smells is an invitation to disobedience and its repercussions.

Our struggle with temptation can be rather exhausting, but that doesn't mean the struggle is without merit. In a way, I think we're *privileged* to be tempted. Wayne Oates, in his definitive book on temptation, wrote, "God created us in an order of creation in which the testing of our mettle as human beings is inevitable. Our creation thrusts us into a process in which we grow and mature."[3]

In chapter 1, I addressed how the testing of our faith through stress-producing trials will create perseverance and maturity. The same is true of temptation. It's like the old cartoon where the main character is faced with a choice, and the tiny angel and devil appear on either side to persuade him one way or the other.[4] Every time those proverbial angels and demons perch on our shoulders and plead with us to agree with them, believers are given an opportunity that the rest of God's creation will never know. We are given the chance to overcome.

The apostle Peter wrote to the Christians in Asia Minor, teaching them that they should be holy as God is holy (see 1 Pet. 1:15-16). If I understand Peter correctly, God *expects* this to happen. God expects holiness from His people, demanding that we think, speak and act differently from the rest of this world. He has entrusted us with His grace, a gift more precious than the stockpiled gold in the Vatican; and because of this, we should live differently. Our lives "post-grace" cannot be the same as "pre-grace." We must become better, even holy. But this definitely will not take place overnight. "Holiness is a process, not a product," Christian psychologist Earl Wilson writes. "As we go through the process, we thank God for our victories and we confess our failures and defeats. Starting over is a daily occurrence. We must constantly crawl back onto the path in pursuit of the holy life God demands."[5]

As we pursue the type of life God calls us to live—despite all the self-help books, daytime television success stories, and well-intentioned diets—we still find ourselves doing the very things we wished we were not doing. Even the apostle Paul struggled with this internal conflict:

> I do not understand what I do. For what I want to do I do not do, but what I hate I do. . . . For I know that good itself does not dwell in me, that is, in my sinful nature.

For I have the desire to do what is good, but I cannot carry it out. For I do not do the good I want to do, but the evil I do not want to do—this I keep on doing (Rom. 7:15,18-19).

You see, there are a lot of ups and downs on the journey toward holiness. Your success lies in recognizing that if you're a Christian, the Holy Spirit lives inside of you, making you holy (see 1 Cor. 6:19). Since the Holy Spirit lives within, you are moved to shed your sinfulness like a dirty jacket and clothe yourself instead in "compassion, kindness, humility, gentleness and patience" (Col. 3:12). And you are empowered to resist the temptation that comes your way, if you do not quench the Holy Spirit's gentle but compelling voice.

Unlike an episode of ABC's *Desperate Housewives* in which the women on Wisteria Lane enrapture audiences by the various ways they give in to temptation, you and I must have higher ambitions. So how do we combat temptation? How can we effectively choose the path toward holiness? If it's true that we're all tempted and that all temptation is common to man, are there some apps we could download from Scripture to use during times of testing? Yes, there are! James 1:13-27 contains excellent examples of how to best overcome temptation and place yourself in the direction toward holiness.

In this chapter, I'd like to present this application to you in six steps, all of which can assist you in the mission of conquering temptation in your life.

**BEGIN DOWNLOAD**

0%　　10%　　20%　　30%　　40%　　50%　　60%　　70%　　80%　　90%

## Step 1: Round Up the Usual Suspects

I recently read an article about the citizens of a small English village who were kept awake at night by a low hum. It would start around midnight and continue until about 4:00 A.M., when it reportedly would disappear. The villagers attempted to describe it as sort of a buzzing or throbbing noise, kind of like an idling diesel engine. The problem was that they had no idea from where this hum was coming. They believed it was coming from outside the village since groups of people and not just a few individuals could hear it. Some postulated that it was merely a faulty electrical line; others assumed it was the rumbling of an abandoned mineshaft; while others thought it was the nearby crashing of the ocean waves. Many were convinced that it was the result of government testing or even the work of UFOs. Regardless, no one could find the source of the problem, and it was driving these villagers mad.

An expert in the field of human hearing examined the mysterious hum in this English village and theorized that the problem wasn't with the village; it was with the people. He concluded that the perceived noise probably occurred when people focused on innocent nighttime noises, which allowed them to grow louder and louder in their minds. "It becomes a vicious cycle," he told the BBC. "The more people focus on the noise, the more anxious and fearful they get, the more the body responds by amplifying the sound, and that causes even more upset and distress."[6]

In a way, I think we can relate to this story. Detecting the origin of temptation's attack becomes about as difficult as locating a mystery hum. We search high and low, yet we are never really sure from where it's coming. Sometimes it's quite obvious, staring us directly in the face. But at other times, it attempts to sneak up on us undetected. Like the captain of a sinking ship, in order to stop the rising water, you need to find the leak—because if you don't find the source of the problem, you're . . . well, sunk.

Oftentimes, we attribute temptation to Satan himself. After all, the story of Jesus' temptation shows us just that. Yet, I think we can go overboard and attribute all temptation in our lives to the great Deceiver. It's true that there are demonic forces at work in this world, blatantly launching their fiery darts of deception or cunningly whispering in our ears. But surprisingly, as we will soon see, even Satan himself is not completely responsible for those times when we are tempted to sin.

Let's go in the other direction. Would it be too far of a stretch to say that God Himself is the one who tempts us? I've actually heard this theory before, and I've seen it played out in hundreds of hospital rooms. A family huddled around the bed of an ailing patient struggles to understand why such pain has been introduced into their lives.

In these instances, I hear the grieving individuals ask, "Why is God doing this to us?" "Why is He testing us?" "Why is He tempting our faith?"

*Does* God tempt us?

The answer is an emphatic no! By no means! James writes in 1:13, "When tempted, no one should say, 'God is tempting me.' For God cannot be tempted by evil, nor does he tempt anyone." It cannot be made any clearer from this passage that temptation and evil do not come from the Lord. He is not in the business of sending misfortune; He is in the business of sending blessings and rewards. And He certainly is not in the business of sending death; He is in the business of giving life.

But during times of difficulty, when our faith moves away from God, it seems like the best option is to blame someone else. When Adam sinned, he blamed Eve. And when Eve sinned, she blamed the Snake. We can blame God or Satan, these otherworldly beings, for our anger or misery. But more often than not, we ourselves are the ones to blame. James continues in 1:14, "Each one is tempted when, by his own evil desire, he is dragged away and enticed."

It is much like the English villagers who reported the inexplicable nighttime noise. The people wanted to blame caves, electrical wires and alien spacecraft; but by far, the most likely explanation was that these residents were creating the clamor themselves. Temptation has a way of doing just that: convincing us to blame someone or something else while we continue to magnify the problem, allowing temptation to grow and fester like a weed until it's unmanageable. This is what James endeavors to teach us in this text: Much of the temptation we endure in our lives is *self-inflicted*.

Jeremiah 17:9 states, "The heart is deceitful above all things," and the only thing the heart can deceive is itself. Oates writes that "self-deception is the parent evil of all temptation."[7] Succumbing to temptation begins when we deceive ourselves and allow our desires to create unreal fantasies about life: that we won't really die; that we have no limits; that we are the exceptions to rules and laws; that we, *not God*, know what is best for us. And when we allow these deceptive thoughts to take root, they transform into the sins that we are so desperately trying to avoid.

The point is that when we round up the usual suspects in an attempt to find the source of our frustration, we should point the finger at ourselves. Accepting the blame—and choosing to react *differently* toward that temptation than we have in the past—enables us to begin to successfully resist that which tempts us. In this way, we set foot on the path toward holiness.

**DOWNLOAD IN PROGRESS**

■■■■■■■■■■■■■□□□□□□□□□□□□□□□□□□□□□□□□□□□□□□□□□□□□□□□□

0%      10%      20%      30%      40%      50%      60%      70%      80%      90%

## Step 2: Consider the Consequences

Now that we've recognized that everyone faces temptation and we've figured out where the temptation comes from, what keeps us from giving in to these enticements? One way is simply to consider the stakes involved in conceding to temptation—to look down the road to see where our actions would place us.

I'm reminded of a story about Harry Truman (not the former president of the United States). This Harry Truman was a store-owner who, in 1980, lived along the beautiful Spirit Lake along the rim of Mount St. Helens, Washington. Yes, you can see where this is going. In the days before Mount St. Helens' eruption on May 18, 1980, both state officials and federal officials pleaded with Harry Truman to leave the premises. Seismologists came to his doorstep and did their best to explain that his house would be in the direct path of an avalanche once the volcano exploded. Two fifth-grade classes sent a bundle of letters to him. One letter from a student in Oregon read, "I know what would happen if lava came out of the volcano and I was there. I would die. Well, bye-bye." Truman decided that he would visit the Oregon class once the heat from the mountain died down. Unfortunately, Harry Truman died in the volcano eruption.[8]

Living in the midst of sin is like living on the side of a volcano that is about to blow. We can live our entire lives confident that nothing will happen and we'll be just fine, but trust me when I write that failing to recognize the dire consequences of sin in your life may have an eternal price tag.

James writes, "After desire has conceived, it gives birth to sin; and sin, when it is full-grown, gives birth to death" (Jas. 1:15). This is the destructive pattern of committing sins: First, we deceive ourselves and listen to the inner desires that war against God's purposes for us; by listening to those desires, we convince ourselves to act against God's will; and by acting against God's will, we place ourselves on a path that takes us further and further away from God and increasingly closer to destruction. (Then, rinse and repeat.)

In Romans 6:21, the apostle Paul tried to reason with the Christians in Rome: "What benefit did you reap at that time from the things you are now ashamed of? Those things result in death!" Sin ends in death. We see this story played out consistently on the news. A drunk driver crashes into the median on a highway, endangering not only his life, but also the lives of others. An unfaithful partner drives the other to financial or relational ruin. A bitter man allows his anger to boil over and resolves to settle his frustrations with violence. A gambler sits at a roulette table, at the expense of his child's college fund. A drug addict steals money from her friends and family in order to fund her chemical bondage. These are merely earthly representations of what is happening in the spiritual realm. People all over this world are choosing a life of sin that leads to death over a life of following Christ that leads to life and holiness. We need to be fully aware of the consequences of succumbing to temptation.

South African bishop Desmond Tutu highlighted the consequences of sin when he wrote, "For the sinner the price is alienation. Sin opens a chasm between the sinner and God. That distance is anathema to God. God does not see only our sin. God sees the good that has been covered up, distorted, blurred by our misdeeds."[9]

The ultimate consequence of sin and rejection of God is an eternity apart from Him; these choices also forever obscure the good we could have done in this life and erase the person we could have been in Christ. Deuteronomy 32:29 reads, "If only they were wise and would understand this and discern what their end will be!" In order to download the next step toward this app, we must possess wisdom and foresight regarding the consequences of our sin.

Have you ever wondered why young children sometimes act with reckless abandon? It is because they cannot foresee the consequences of their actions. They can only see what's happening right now; they are too busy to be troubled with the realities of the future. And yet, do we not act in the same way when we seek the instant gratification and momentary pleasure that sin affords? We fixate on the present, on what makes us feel good now, and forget that there is an eternity waiting for us on the other side of death. We'll either spend eternity with God the Father, or we'll spend it apart from Him.

**DOWNLOAD IN PROGRESS**

| 0% | 10% | 20% | 30% | 40% | 50% | 60% | 70% | 80% | 90% |

## Step 3: Stock Up on Left Tackles

Michael Lewis's inspiring work *The Blindside,* the story of how Michael Oher succeeded from homelessness on the streets of Memphis to the offensive line of the NFL football team of the Baltimore Ravens, may not have been written were it not for defensive players such as Reggie White. An ordained minister off the field, Reggie White was known as the "Minister of Defense" on the field. Why? Because White was a two-time NFL defensive player of the year and led the league in career sacks when he retired after the 2000 season. (Bruce Smith has since surpassed his record.)[10] A defensive player like White made the opposing offensive position of "left tackle" one of the most important positions in football. Whenever White blitzed, hoping to catch the quarterback from behind and waylay him like an enraged rhinoceros, the offensive left tackle was the one who would try to stop him. The left tackle protected the quarterback's weak spot, ensuring his safety and their team's victory.

It's of utmost importance to acquire a good left tackle on an NFL roster, especially since there are a multitude of terrifying defensive linemen out there who would love nothing more than to shove a quarterback's helmet into the turf. In the same way, it's not always easy to defend against our human desires. It's almost as if we're the quarterback, ready to pull back and fire a pass for a touchdown, yet our body is screaming out to fall to the ground and end the play. It's like we're trying to sack ourselves. Combine that with the demonic forces blitzing toward our weaknesses and attempting to finish the job. That makes for a difficult scenario.

How can we begin to rebuff temptation's advances? We must know our weaknesses. We may be able to sense our sinful urges flaring up, and we may be able to carefully assess the situation, understanding the consequences of our actions, but we won't get far unless we know the areas in which we are vulnerable.

When Satan tempted Jesus, he attacked the areas where he could do the most damage (see Matt. 4:1-11). First, he launched his assault on Jesus' humanity. It had been 40 days and nights since Jesus had eaten anything, so Satan's first order of business was to remind Jesus that, as the Son of God, He could quickly put an end to His own hunger. When that temptation failed, Satan changed his ploy by transporting Jesus to the highest point of the temple and asking Him to take the leap, hoping that Jesus would doubt His faith in the Father and put it to the test. Having lost on that front as well, the devil decided to offer everything that Jesus could possibly want on a silver platter: all the glorious kingdoms of the world. All Jesus had to do was bow down and worship Satan. Above all, the devil sought to overthrow the crucifixion and all that it would accomplish in God's epic story, and so he attempted to strike Jesus at His weakest points and derail His mission. In the same way, temptation seeks to gain victory over us by striking us at the weak places in our spiritual armor that can easily lead us to succumb to temptation, such as anger, lust, unforgiveness or greed.

How do you find your weaknesses? Start by asking your close friends. Trust me, they'll know. Consult with the people in the church with whom you have the closest relationship, and ask them to watch your back by helping to hold you accountable in your weak areas. Christianity is a team effort, and there's no reason why any of us should attempt to fight this battle alone. Think of it as driving in heavy traffic with a group of friends in the car. When you need to make a lane change, you can check your blind spot by turning your head around to look; but in that moment, you're taking your eyes off the road in front of you. In a car full of friends, it's much easier to ask them to check for you. It may seem a little awkward at first, but it's definitely safer. And it's safer in our Christian lives to ask our friends to assess our weaknesses, because they'll catch what we often fail to see.

Daily journaling and reflection are also especially effective in identifying areas of weakness. By slowing down and thinking about what has happened in the day, or reading about it months or years after it happened, you can look back with hindsight and continue to improve your defenses against temptation.

One last thought: If you spend too much time focusing on your weaknesses, you should not think it's beyond your enemy to attack your strengths. Though Moses was considered the meekest man in the Bible, he was tempted to be prideful, trusting in his own strength rather than in God's when he struck the rock with his rod and caused water to flow for the Israelites (see Num. 20:7-12). Samson was the strongest man in the Bible, but he was not able to control his lust (see Judg. 16). David was considered a man after God's own heart, but he gave in to his desire for another man's wife, and in order to cover up his sin, sent the man to be killed in battle (see 2 Sam. 11). Peter, in his boldness, swore he would follow Jesus to the death, but after Christ was arrested, the impulsive apostle quickly denied his Lord three times when confronted by others about his association with Jesus (see Luke 22:33-34,56-57). There's no question that you and I must be vigilant and keep our eyes on the road, checking both our weak blind spots and our strong areas so that we don't wind up in a disastrous collision.

**DOWNLOAD IN PROGRESS**

0%    10%    20%    30%    40%    50%    60%    70%    80%    90%

## Step 4: Clean Out the Cupboard

I once read an article about a couple that purchased a five-bedroom home in Idaho. From the outset, it looked like a great deal. They were purchasing the house for a cheap price on a good stretch of land. As far as they were concerned, they had purchased their dream home for the years to come. But it didn't take them long to discover why the house sold so cheaply. The house was infested with garter snakes—hundreds of them.

One of the owners quipped that at times the infestation got so bad, when they looked outside, the ground looked like it was moving. During the night, they could hear slithering in the walls. In one day, the husband claimed to have killed 42 snakes. (Have I freaked you out yet?)

I couldn't imagine living like that, and neither could the owners. They declared bankruptcy and promptly moved out. The husband admitted that he had been diagnosed with snake-related post-traumatic stress disorder.[11]

I use this story to illustrate a very important point in your fight against temptation: You cannot live in a house full of snakes. Either you or the snakes must go. What do I mean? If you struggle with pornography, you cannot keep your computer in a secluded room without some type of accountability software installed. If you have difficulty controlling your drinking, you cannot keep alcohol in your house or frequent bars and clubs. If you have anger-related issues, you cannot watch violent movies or listen to music that indulges or inflames your anger. You may also want to refrain from competitive sports. If you are obsessed with gossip, stop lounging around the water cooler, and turn off TMZ.

You can't live in a house of snakes.

It's time to empty the cupboard of the things that tempt you. When you have properly identified your weaknesses, the next step is to ensure that temptation has a difficult time getting to those weaknesses. Paul urges us in Ephesians 4:27, "Do not give the devil a foothold." Translation: Do your utmost to eliminate any chance of either the devil or your own evil desires grabbing hold of any corner of your life and climbing further into your heart to bend it to his will.

I believe this was at the heart of James's message to his community when he wrote in 1:19-20, "Everyone should be quick to listen, slow to speak and slow to become angry, for man's anger does not bring about the righteous life that God desires." Anger can be a gateway sin leading to other more destructive sins. Anger floods our senses, blinds us to the truth of a given situation and deceives us to act against God's purposes. It cannot produce the holy life God desires from us.

Giving temptation a foothold may seem harmless at first; it almost always starts small. But if we allow that temptation to fester in our lives, it can become much more difficult to handle than we initially anticipated. My father uses an anecdote that illustrates this truth. It is about a street performer who used a snake in his show. He would place the snake in a tree and then give it a command to come down from the tree and wrap itself around him. The snake would writhe its way up the man's body and stare directly at him. The crowd grew concerned until the performer gave another command, causing the snake to unwrap its body from the performer and climb back into the tree. The people couldn't get enough of this act.

Eventually, he drew quite a crowd. One night, the air had a strange electricity about it. The performer went about his routine as usual, commanding the snake to come down from the tree and wrap itself around him. But as he commanded the snake to unwrap itself from his body, the snake started squeezing. He ordered the snake to retreat, but it didn't, continuing to squeeze him. The audience was unaware of what was happening as they watched the man get crushed to death right in front of them.

A newspaper reporter attended the performer's funeral to record the events of the evening. He noticed a man sitting on a curb, openly weeping. The reporter asked this man if he happened to be a friend of the deceased. He replied, "Yes, I was his friend, and I told him countless times to get rid of that snake! I knew that if he didn't, one day that snake would turn on him!"

As the reporter recorded his words, the man added, "I remember the day he ordered that snake like it was yesterday. It came in a box in the mail. When he opened the box, I remember that he held the snake in the palm of his hand. It was so small that he could have crushed it right then. But he didn't. He allowed it to grow, and now it has taken his life."

When our sins are minuscule and manageable, we can allow ourselves to be deceived or deny their effect on us. *We can handle it*, we say. But trust me when I say that we should crush those "harmless" sins as soon as possible. If not, they grow into something much more overwhelming and will eventually squeeze the life out of us.

**DOWNLOAD IN PROGRESS**

0%   10%   20%   30%   40%   50%   60%   70%   80%   90%

## Step 5: Develop Your Green Thumb

You've taken every possible precaution to guard against succumbing to temptation. The next step is to face the temptation at hand and fight back. The key is to *resist*. James later writes in his letter, "Resist the devil and he will flee from you" (4:7). The same is true of temptation. Stand up and resist the urge, and it will subside.

Sometimes, those desires will not immediately disappear. Instead, they'll park in the back of your mind and wait, building strength like a wave that swells until its size completely engulfs you. What do you do then?

Here is James's advice: "Humbly accept the word planted in you, which can save you" (1:21). I love the imagery of that phrase: "The word *planted* in you." It evokes the image of a sturdy oak tree, firmly planted and anchored by deep roots, which does not bow or bend even in the face of the strongest wind or most tumultuous storm. This is how God's Word should exist in our minds—as a refuge of safety from temptation's assault. Such imagery of the power of God's Word in combatting temptation is also seen in Paul's description of the armor of God in Ephesians 6:10-17. The armor of God *protects us* "against the powers of this dark world and against the spiritual forces of evil in the heavenly realms" (v. 12) and *enables us* to "extinguish all the flaming arrows of the *evil one*" (v. 16, emphasis added). The only weapon included in this armor is "the sword of the Spirit, which is the word of God" (v. 17).

The 176-verse opus in Psalm 119 arrests our senses with vivid imagery about the importance of the Word of God. We read that Scripture is "more precious than thousands of pieces of silver and gold" (v. 72), "sweeter than honey to my mouth" (v. 103), and acts as "a lamp to my feet and a light to my path" (v. 105). In the life of the psalmist, Scripture's significance was incalculable.

If there were ever a charge given to Christians, it would surely be to know more Scripture. Knowing God's Word inside and out should be a primary objective for *every* Christian, because having a good handle on Scripture is essential to tackle our temptations. For example, the apostle Paul describes the life-changing purpose of God's Word to Timothy, a young believer: "All Scripture is God-breathed and is useful for teaching, rebuking, correcting and training in righteousness, so that the servant of God may be thoroughly equipped for every good work" (2 Tim. 3:16-17). Therefore, it is through the continued study and increasing knowledge of God's Word that not only can we stand firm against temptation, but we can also learn about and be trained in righteousness.

This training requires that we dig deep—making the commitment to study the Bible every single day. This discipline is what strengthens us spiritually and enables us to overcome temptation.

However, when we look at God's Word, we may think that there is too much information and that our mind isn't capable of retaining everything. We may convince ourselves that we shouldn't bother even trying!

I can tell you that in many years of ministry, I have read the Bible from cover to cover, but I definitely cannot remember everything I've read. That's not necessarily the goal. Sure, we need to come away from our study of Scripture with knowledge that can help us combat temptation; but more to the point, when we take part in God's Word, we are cleansing ourselves in God's Scripture. In Ephesians 5:26, Paul uses the image of "washing," which indicates that the Word cleanses us.

Imagine placing a colander or strainer under your kitchen faucet and allowing water to run through it. How much water would that utensil retain? Maybe a few droplets at best. However, this would not be a pointless exercise because something important is happening as the water flows through the colander: Though it's not containing any of the water, its impurities are being washed away.

Similarly, when you read God's Word, you may think that you're not retaining much, but an invaluable cleansing of your soul is taking place. We wouldn't necessarily remember everything we read, nor can we. John Ortberg says it this way: "To be filled with knowledge about the Bible, but to be unwashed by it is worse than not knowing it at all. . . . The goal is not for us to get through the Scriptures. The goal is to get the Scriptures through us."[12] That's why studying God's Word is a lifelong process. We will never know enough about Scripture. Just ask any theologian or biblical scholar worth his or her salt. The point is to approach the Bible with an open heart and allow its cleansing to take place. In doing so, we will uproot temptation's weeds and cultivate the Word of God, which has been planted in us. (For a fun and easy way to get your daily dose of God's Word, download the Bible in a Year app onto your smartphone. Click on the "Bible in a Year" icon on the homepage of www.GodHasAn App.com to learn more.)

**DOWNLOAD IN PROGRESS**

0%　10%　20%　30%　40%　50%　60%　70%　80%　90%

## Step 6: Go on the Offensive

The final step toward downloading God's app to overcome temptation is found in James 1:22: "Do not merely listen to the word, and so deceive yourselves. Do what it says." Said simply, live out the Word. We cannot merely let the Word wash over us. We must go even further by allowing it to well up in our soul and burst out like a fire hydrant, dousing temptation and sin with the cleansing power of God's truth.

It doesn't help to merely know what the Word says if that Word never manifests itself in your actions. Author Francis Chan tells a story about instructing his daughter to go clean her room. She leaves for a bit, and then comes back with a big smile across her face. "Did you do what I asked?" Francis asks his daughter.

"I did exactly what you wanted me to," she replied. "I memorized your command, 'Go, clean your room.' I studied it in Greek to figure out the original meaning of 'Go, clean your room,' and I'm going to have my friends come over and discuss what it means to 'Go, clean your room.' "[13]

Now, you and I both know that Francis didn't intend that his daughter memorize his command, and we can surmise that he didn't want her to study the ancient Greek meaning of the word "clean." He just wanted her to go and clean her room. Like Francis's daughter, sometimes we forget that what God expects is for us to live out His commands. We act as if talking about or studying His commands is all that God wants from us. James compares such ineffectual "study" to someone who is dismissive about his or her appearance: "Anyone who listens to the word but does not do what it says is like someone who looks at his face in a mirror and, after looking at himself, goes away and immediately forgets what he looks like" (Jas. 1:23-24). It's true that the *first* thing we are quick to correct in ourselves is anything that improves our physical appearance. However, how quick are we to rectify sin in our lives when God's Word reveals it to us?

Bible studies and Scripture reading are designed not just to give us a bundle of information, but also to transform us into holy followers of Christ. James goes on to explain that "whoever looks intently into the perfect law that gives freedom, and continues in it—not forgetting what they have heard, but doing it—they will be blessed in what they do" (v. 25).

This is the final stage of combatting temptation, the moment when this fight switches from defense to offense. Christianity is *proactive*. We often define our Christianity by what we abstain from instead of by what we accomplish. Following Jesus is not just about maintaining holiness. It's about taking action. The Pharisees in Jesus' day believed that the path to heaven was paved in strict observance of God's Law. If they could keep God's laws perfectly, they would be saved. This is why they would rarely mingle with the poor, the sick, the Gentile and other outcasts in the Jewish community. They kept themselves at arm's length from the "sinners," because to be grouped with them was to jeopardize their salvation.

Jesus described "perfection" not in terms of how many laws His followers could keep, but by how far their love actively reached others (see Matt. 5:43-48). Christianity is not a passing interest for study. It is an entire way of life meant to penetrate and transform the world around us. While we must be vigilant toward temptation's ploys, this does not mean that we must keep the rest of the world at arm's length. Instead, we should live with our arms open wide to those who are looking for help in order to bring healing into their lives.

The best part is that when we actively show God's love and forgiveness to others, we are taking the fight to temptation's lair. If you struggle with greed, then volunteer at a homeless shelter and make friends with people who have survived on nothing. If anger lurks in your life, get involved in an anger management program where you could later mentor others. Do you struggle with pride? Volunteer to do yard work, fold church bulletins, sort clothing or clean toilets. Do you wrestle with envy or coveting others' possessions? Donate to organizations working in third-world countries or go on a short-term mission trip to impoverished areas of the world.

In these cases, we allow God to turn our weaknesses into strengths, recognizing God's words to the apostle Paul when he said, "My power is made perfect in weakness" (2 Cor. 12:9). In the midst of our weakness and frailty—in the areas where we seem most vulnerable—God is willing and able to begin a new work in us, using our former disappointments and shame as prime opportunities for Christian growth. From our weakness, God's love shines.

I often tell people who are struggling with temptation to keep a Bible in their hand at all times. I've received some furrowed brows and questioning stares from that little tidbit of advice, but honestly, it works. The man tempted to view pornography cannot do so with a Bible in his hand. The woman enticed to overspend in a clothing store cannot fish out the credit card with the Holy Scriptures in her clutches. The student will be hard-pressed to cheat on an exam while one hand firmly grasps a Bible. And if your problems with temptation are so extreme that holding a Bible isn't enough to stop it, then carry *two* Bibles—one in each hand! You might look silly, but you need to do whatever it takes to battle the temptations that arise from your own desires.

When we actively seek to live out God's Word, temptation will look less appealing to us. I love the story of an Okinawan village named Shimabuku, which American forces discovered during World War II. At the entrance of the town stood two men who bowed low to the troops and identified themselves as Christians. One of the men held a tattered Bible in his hand. As the troops toured the village, they noticed how different the townspeople seemed. Normally, the Okinawans were dejected and morose when American troops came, but these people were warm and inviting. Their homes were pristine, their fields fertile and they even had a successful sugar mill.

Finally, one of the troops asked about the history of this village. One of the elders explained that a long while ago, a Christian missionary had appeared and spent a short time in the village. During his stay, he converted two men in the village to Christianity, left them with a Japanese translation of the Bible and taught them a few hymns before leaving. They had not met another Christian since.

The people of the village immersed themselves in the Bible and came to the conclusion that Jesus Christ was Lord. Furthermore, they found in the Word of God commands that were a suitable pattern for their community. The Ten Commandments served as their law, and the Sermon on the Mount modeled their social conduct. In the local school, the Bible was the primary instructional resource the children studied.

Here's the kicker: This village had no jail, no brothel, no drunkenness and no divorce.[14] Can you believe that? None! I look at this story, and I wonder what would happen if we placed God's Word at the center of our lives and modeled our laws and social conduct on it. Would our society be anything like the village of Shimabuku? I'm sure that temptation would have a difficult time finding a foothold in such a community.

**DOWNLOAD COMPLETE!**

0%   10%   20%   30%   40%   50%   60%   70%   80%   90%

In this chapter, you've discovered six steps in the process of downloading God's app for overcoming temptation. They are:

- Identify the source of temptation, ultimately discovering that it is often the result of our own desires.
- Step back and weigh the consequences before succumbing to temptation. When you allow sin to take hold of your life, you are jeopardizing an eternity with Christ (see Matt 7:21-23; Heb. 10:26-29).
- Know your weaknesses, because these are the points at which temptation will strike.
- Clean out everything in your life that could possibly let Satan gain a foothold and cause you to fall.
- Know God's Word. Memorize key passages of Scripture, which can help you to repel daily temptations.

• Go on the offensive and actively fight temptation by being obedient to the principles taught in God's Word.

The key to overcoming temptation is to thoroughly know God's Word and use it to fill your mind and direct your actions. When Jesus withstood the devil's tricks, He did so each time by responding with a verse from Scripture.

"Aren't you hungry?" Satan asked.

Jesus replied, "It is written: 'Man does not live on bread alone, but on every word that comes from the mouth of God'" (Matt. 4:4). He got that from Deuteronomy 8:3.

"Prove that you're God's Son," Satan demanded.

Jesus answered, "It is also written: 'Do not put the Lord your God to the test'" (Matt. 4:7). This warning is found in Deuteronomy 6:16.

"I can give you what you want," Satan lied. "Just bow down and worship me."

Without breaking a sweat, Jesus quoted, "It is written: 'Worship the Lord your God, and serve him only" (Matt. 4:10) from Deuteronomy 6:13.

With firsthand experience of the enemy's most enticing schemes, Jesus demonstrated a surefire way to achieve victory in the face of temptation—by reciting Scripture. There's no other way to be able to quote the Word at any given moment than by reading the Bible every single day and letting it permeate your being. Like listening to your favorite song over and over again, daily time in God's Word will get it into your heart and mind and come out of your mouth in the most critical situations. We can know this is a system that works, because Christ was "tempted in every way, just as we are—yet he did not sin" (Heb. 4:15).

God Has an App to
# Break Down the Walls that Divide

## James 2:1-12

Cliques. Popularity. Sports teams formed on the basis of athleticism and likability. Teacher's pet. Favored sibling. Do any of these words conjure up flashbacks from your childhood? The sort of favoritism that introduces itself so early in life may bring back bitter memories. I remember being teased just because of my first name: "The Dud," "Milk Dud," "Dudley Do Right," "Dudley Do Something!" Kids can be both clever and cruel. And those feelings of being unpopular, a "geek" or the "ugly duckling" are quick to remind us how we were labeled or treated as children—and how charmed, special and popular our peers seemed to be.

Favoritism wasn't limited to the halls of our high schools after we graduated. We found that it flourishes everywhere. It burrows into the business arena, sneaks into sports and lingers in our families. What's more, favoritism is actually glamorized by the entertainment world and is manifested in rather odd ways, when you think about it.

Having lived in Los Angeles for the past 20 years, I have seen the seemingly universal obsession with "celebrity culture" up close.

Every time a limousine drives by, you can't help but wonder what prominent person its tinted windows conceal. An enchanted face on the cover of nationwide tabloids may very well be the same person ordering a latte ahead of you at the local coffee shop. The streets you walk are literally imprinted with the names of everyone who's "anyone" in this city, and many of us tend to think in terms of "VIP" and "General Admittance" in classifying people.

In America, the elitism we were either a part of or excluded from in high school can appear in other subtle ways in adulthood. We favor those who possess our ideal economic status or like the same sports teams that we like or share our political views.

Just a few weekends ago, I had the opportunity to officiate the marriage ceremony for a lovely couple. Usually, the bride's loved ones sit on one side of the aisle while the groom's family sits on the other. But at this particular event, there were a few more underlying divisions, because the bride was an African-American actress working in liberal Hollywood, and her groom was a Caucasian news correspondent working for a conservative television network.

As I stood with the groom, waiting for the beautiful bride to make her entrance, I couldn't help but peruse the audience and realize that the only thing everyone had in common was their desire to witness this couple's wedding. I couldn't help but sense the polite yet unseen walls separating black and white, young and old, liberal and conservative. Even at such a joyous occasion, favoritism showed up like an unwanted guest.

This unwelcome visitor makes a weekly appearance in churches across the United States. God's Word, in James 2:1-12, sheds light upon favoritism's infiltration of the church, as we will soon find out. But first let's examine what favoritism is and why it is so detrimental to our faith and to society.

## What Is Favoritism?

Favoritism is "to have a favorable bias toward one person or group over others with equal claims."[1] It may seem harmless enough at first. You may prefer the Lakers to the Celtics, or Republicans over

Democrats, or those who wear Nike to those who wear Adidas. But seemingly innocuous preferences quickly become prejudices based on a number of other external factors, such as social class, disability, gender, race, physical appearance and cultural differences. A foreign accent, an inexpensive car, a wheelchair or a shade of skin may lead one to make unfair judgments about another person, even before you exchange a simple "hello." And that is why favoritism is such a problem. It fosters an "us versus them" attitude of superiority that constructs invisible walls among fellow human beings—walls that divide.

Moreover, this inclination directly defies God's will for His people, as James points out: "My brothers and sisters, believers in our glorious Lord Jesus Christ must not show favoritism" (Jas. 2:1). Here, James specifically identifies the sinful tendency to treat someone differently due to financial status.

I don't care who you are, when you see a person of a particular economic or social status, it's hard not to treat him or her differently. I'm aware of it in my own church. Whenever a millionaire or a movie star walks into our lobby or worship service, everyone stands a little taller and smiles a little wider as if they are hoping to catch the favored person's eye. I like to think we have a friendly and welcoming church, but we almost become an effervescent musical number from a scene on Broadway when a wealthy, successful or famous person strolls in. I've even seen Grumpy Gunther or Sour Sally give up his or her seat in the front row—the seats upon which they've staked claim for the past 15 years—to Marvin Millionaire or Monica Movie Star.

Friend, walls constructed by favoritism and prejudice must be torn down if we aspire to reflect the heart of the living God and have a genuine relationship with Him and with others. The barrier of favoritism may be old, strong, high, wide and thick, but it is not impenetrable. In fact, through the words recorded in James 2, God offers an app to break down any wall that divides us, and build up unity and love.

I pray that in fully downloading this app, we will effectively combat attitudes that have compromised the true character of the

Christian cause. I wholeheartedly believe that in eliminating favoritism, through the power of God's Word, our lives, our churches, our nation and our world will be transformed. Ready to download? Good! Let's get started. This app contains six key points that will enable you to boldly break down the walls that divide

**BEGIN DOWNLOAD**

0%    10%    20%    30%    40%    50%    60%    70%    80%    90%

## Step 1: Slather On the Oil

Have you ever studied all the uses for oil? I don't mean Crisco, Pennzoil 10w30, or the kind in the Middle East that everyone always seems to be fighting over. I mean the good ol' natural stuff like olive oil, or the Omega-3, -6 and -9 essential fatty acids found in our bodies and in the good-for-you fish, like wild salmon. There are a *ton* of great benefits to this kind of oil! Indulge my excitement for just a moment as I highlight three of its most wonderful applications.

First, oil lubricates. If your mind instantly returned to the thought of Pennzoil making its way through a car's engine and causing everything to run smoothly, that's fine; it's sort of like that in the human body. The good kind of oil—that nuts, fish and avocado offer—is essential for your cardiovascular health and the lubrication of your joints. It also enriches your hair and skin, making them shiny and smooth as it fights against brittleness and dryness. If you were to eliminate all fat and oil from your diet, you'd be walking around stiffer and drier than a dead leaf.

Second, oil heals. Grape seed, tea tree, oregano, borage, evening primrose and flax seed oils are *not* ingredients you'd find in a witch's cupboard. These oils can be purchased at any health food store, and they contain amazing healing properties for all kinds of skin ailments. For example, borage oil and evening primrose oil can relieve the itch accompanied by eczema; tea tree oil contains antifungal properties to help combat athlete's foot and ringworm. Author Philip Keller argues that when King

David wrote, in Psalm 23, "the Lord is my Shepherd" who "anoints my head with oil," he was referencing a shepherd's tendency to apply a mixture of oil with various herbs on the wounds of his sheep to heal irritation, counter infection and keep away pesky flies.[2]

Finally, and most important for our application today, oil repels water. Many animals—such as sea lions, otters, ducks and certain water-loving dogs—produce extra oil in their skin that repels water. Car wax contains oil to keep water from collecting on a car's shiny, clean exterior. Certain hair products boast that they can prevent your hair from succumbing to humidity, and that's because they contain natural or synthetic oils. I can't really say whether or not they actually work, since I'm a bit lacking in the hair department!

But if you've ever tried to combine water and oil in a clear glass, you've seen how the oil will instantly separate itself from the water in languid bubbles that bounce around the container. When James makes this heartfelt plea, "My brothers, believers in our glorious Lord Jesus Christ must not show favoritism," he is saying that being a Christian and showing favoritism are like oil and water—unmixable!

The reason for this is that in placing our faith in the Lord, His Spirit dwells within us and we are motivated to become like Him (see 1 Pet. 1:15-16) and reflect His nature. God's nature can be summarized in four glorious letters: L-O-V-E. John 3:16 tells us that God "so loved the *world* that he gave his one and only Son, that *whoever* believes in him shall not perish but have eternal life" (emphasis added). This exemplary verse, and others such as Isaiah 53:5 and Romans 3:23-24, shows us quite clearly that the Lord's heart is for *all* mankind. Young and old, rich and poor, and every last color of the diverse, human rainbow, God's provision for salvation extends to each and every one of us. And His love is impartial. See for yourself:

- "Therefore go and make disciples of *all nations*" (Matt. 28:19, emphasis added).

- "Then Peter began to speak: 'I now realize how true it is that God does not show favoritism'" (Acts 10:34).
- "For God does not show favoritism" (Rom. 2:11).
- "There is no favoritism with him" (Eph. 6:9).

When you invite God's Spirit to dwell in your heart, what results is a lot like the oily principles we discussed earlier. First, not only will you be lubricated and alive, but you will also bring life to those around you by sharing the joy and hope of the gospel of Jesus Christ. And, like the healing oil placed on the shepherd's lambs, you will help heal the hearts of those who have been snubbed, rejected and cast aside. You will repel favoritism, for it will be impossible for it to co-exist in you! When you slather on the oil, it's the first step in downloading God's app to break down the walls that divide

**DOWNLOAD IN PROGRESS**

0%   10%   20%   30%   40%   50%   60%   70%   80%   90%

## Step 2: Keep an Eye on Favoritism's Cousin!

I was captivated by the sight of half a dozen or so South American piranhas that inhabited a large aquarium in my friend's living room. With sparkling silver scales and bright red bellies, these fish are actually quite exquisite creatures. But when I noticed their trademark underbite displaying ferociously sharp, interlocking teeth, I had to remember that they are highly aggressive aquatic predators that deserve a healthy respect and caution.

As we watched them gliding back and forth through the water, my friend asked, "Do you want to watch them feed?"

"I thought you'd never ask!" was my eager reply.

He grabbed a plastic bag full of live goldfish that were swimming in their encapsulated sea without a care in the world. Up until that moment, life had been good for those goldfish. Then my friend disrupted their peaceful existence by untying the bag and pouring the fish into the hungry piranhas' tank.

What happened next surprised me: The instant the goldfish hit the water, they immediately swam in the opposite direction from the prowling piranhas. It didn't take but the twinkling of an eye for them to figure out they were in enemy territory. No one needed to explain to them that they were in serious trouble, and despite their best efforts, they were devoured in a matter of seconds. The poor little guys never stood a chance.

After watching this would-be Discovery Channel scene unfold, I was amazed by the thought that even one of the smallest and least impressive of fish knows instinctively whether or not it is swimming in friendly waters. If that instinct exists in a goldfish, I can't help but think how much more a human being is aware of his or her surroundings.

You and I must be sensitive to the sometimes unwelcoming or hostile environment of our world caused by a close cousin of favoritism—prejudice. Favoritism is indeed a slippery slope, for it can easily turn into prejudice, and prejudice can morph into racism without any effort at all. So, before continuing through our text in the book of James, I felt it was important to take a brief detour to highlight this divisive force.

Prejudice is defined as "an unfavorable opinion or feeling formed beforehand or without knowledge, thought or reason . . . especially of a hostile nature regarding a racial, religious, or national group."[3] No one is born with prejudicial feelings; they are developed and nurtured within us by our experiences and upbringing. Consider the many factors involved: Babies are born into rich families and poor families alike—each capable of developing resentment toward the other. Children will often adopt prejudicial attitudes from their parents' racist remarks and actions. There are always two sides of the train tracks, with people on each side often unwilling to cross. One negative experience with a person may lead to false stereotyping of an entire people group.

Throughout world history, numerous horrific deeds have been carried out in this spirit. During the eighteenth century, approximately 6 million Africans were captured and transported across the world via the transatlantic slave trade.[4] Between 1915 and 1923, some 1.5 million Armenians perished in the Armenian genocide.[5]

Following Adolf Hitler's rise to power in 1933, it is estimated that 11 million people—6 million of whom were Jews—were systematically captured and executed.[6] "The Holocaust illustrates the consequences of prejudice, racism and stereotyping on a society," said Tim Holden, a member of the U.S. House of Representatives. "It forces us to examine the responsibilities of citizenship and confront the powerful ramifications of indifference and inaction."[7]

Because humanity's history will be forever marked by tragedies such as these, it's important that we do not forget how malignant and destructive prejudice and racism are. Although we are living in the twenty-first century and have made great strides toward fighting these forces, we still have a long way to go. Various prejudices still exist today, wounding hearts and erecting barriers between brethren. In order to begin to break down the walls that divide, we must be sensitive to the fact that these biases are closely related to favoritism.

**DOWNLOAD IN PROGRESS**

0%    10%    20%    30%    40%    50%    60%    70%    80%    90%

## Step 3: Take a Cue from Drizzy

It is often said that dogs are colorblind. In truth, they can see more than just black, white, and gray; however, the color range they perceive is very limited compared to the spectrum humans see.[8] The belief that dogs are colorblind more accurately references their total lack of partiality. Unconcerned about their owners' race, ethnicity, age or socioeconomic status, dogs have no reluctance to love and be loved.

During his third year in college, my son decided to get a dog. A tiny Chihuahua-Miniature Pinscher mix that he purchased for $60 from a family in East Los Angeles captured his heart. He named the pup "Drizzy." Initially, none of us were sure whether Drizzy was a rat or a dog, but he quickly became a special part of our family, as dogs tend to do.

We have joked about Drizzy's innate ability to make you feel like you are the most important person in the world. You could be having the worst day at work, mess up big time on a test or feel crummy after an argument with a loved one; but when you come home to this little canine, he makes you feel like a king or queen! He seems to have mastered Philippians 2:3, which reads, "Do nothing out of selfish ambition or vain conceit. Rather, in humility value others above yourselves." (Imagine all the problems that would be solved if everyone adopted this mindset!)

And it does not matter who you are; when you walk into the room, Drizzy acts as if you're his long-lost love returning from overseas. He will plow through anyone or anything to greet you. Then you'll pick him up and feel his little heart pounding from the excitement of being in your presence. Truly, Drizzy is color-blind. This quality has earned dogs the title of "man's best friend." (To see Drizzy in action, visit the "Videos" section of www.GodHasAnApp.com.)

If only you and I could run to others with the same love and acceptance that Drizzy bestows upon everyone he meets. With this in mind, let us return to James 2:2-4:

> Suppose a man comes into your meeting wearing a gold ring and fine clothes, and a poor man in filthy old clothes also comes in. If you show special attention to the man wearing fine clothes and say, "Here's a good seat for you," but say to the poor man, "You stand there" or "Sit on the floor by my feet," have you not discriminated among yourselves and become judges with evil thoughts?

James is saying that we, like Drizzy, should treat everyone the same way—with kindness, respect and hospitality, regardless of their perceived financial status. But notice that James does not say that we should refrain from *seeing* the differences among people. Don't you think it would be impossible *not* to notice a gold ring and fine clothes on one person, and filthy old clothes

on another person? Thus, James is not admonishing us to go colorblind, for as former U.S. Senator George Aiken once noted, "If
we were to wake up some morning and find that everyone was the
same race, creed and color, we would find some other causes for
prejudice by noon." The issue is not about noticing the differences among people; the issue, as James points out, is about paying "special attention" to those who appear to be rich.

Like a single thread in a brilliant tapestry, an instrument in a
glorious orchestra, or a stroke within a gorgeous painting, so is
each individual on God's created earth. Every shape, size and color
adds to the detail and intricacy of His work. Our similarities and
our differences blend together as a marvelous masterpiece. We
complement, highlight and balance one another.

Since we are equipped with the ability to *see* the differences in
others, not only should we treat everyone equally, but we also
ought to acknowledge and appreciate the elements that make each
person unique. Rather than ignoring or simply tolerating our differences, we should celebrate and delight in them, knowing that
we each are crafted perfectly by the Lord's hand.

I have heard it said that God does not see blindly; He sees
kindly. What this means to me is that our heavenly Father looks at
each of us and appreciates the nuances He created in our appearance, personality and character. Moreover, despite our sin and our
flaws, our grumpiness and the times we've failed to love and bless
others, He looks upon us with kindness and compassion. You can
do the same thing!

Though your tendency may be to stay in your comfort zone,
sticking to what you know and clinging to people who are like you,
have the courage to venture from what feels safe. Favoritism cannot be defeated on a whim. When you see someone who is different from you, be deliberate in delighting in the variety of God's
creation. Each day, remember to take a cue from Drizzy by reaching out to others with joy, enthusiasm and a kind word of encouragement. You will make him or her feel like the most important
person in the world in that moment, and further break down the
wall that divides.

**DOWNLOAD IN PROGRESS**

0%    10%    20%    30%    40%    50%    60%    70%    80%    90%

## Step 4: Give Up the Gavel

Clark Rockefeller was born into great wealth as a member of the Rockefeller dynasty. Though he was estranged from his famous family, those around Clark embraced him and were intrigued by both his past and his personal ambitions. One such person was Sandra Boss. The couple fell in love, got married and enjoyed a prosperous lifestyle through Sandra's high income as a business consultant for a top management firm, while Clark worked on pro-bono cases for underdeveloped countries.[9]

But Clark Rockefeller wasn't a real person. He was simply the alias of a man named Christian Karl Gerhartsreiter, a German immigrant whose many identities through the years included being a doctor and a Pentagon advisor. You see, when Gerhartsreiter moved to the United States as a teenager, he quickly discovered that Americans are intrigued by the rich and the famous. So, he wildly embellished his background to give the impression that he was a member of the Rockefeller family and set out to live the life of a wealthy man. He had an entire city fooled, including his wife of 12 years.[10]

Sadly, you and I are no wiser than those who were duped by Clark the con man. When we see someone walk down the street, into our workplace, in a supermarket or our church, and they're wearing an expensive-looking ring and designer clothing, we automatically assume they must be pretty wealthy and successful. On the highways and byways, we'll see someone driving a fancy car and think, *Wow, they've really got it made.* But the irony is that—especially in America—many people live beyond their means.

Eighty-six percent of all prestige or luxury vehicles are driven by people who are not millionaires.[11] And how many people do you know who are in over their heads with their mortgage payments? We buy clothes we can't afford to wear, purchase cars we can't afford to drive, invest in houses we can't afford to live in and go on vacations we can't afford to enjoy. As Proverbs 13:7 points out, "One pretends to be rich, yet has nothing; another pretends to be poor, yet has great wealth" (*ESV*).

Like Clark Rockefeller, we are very good at fooling others with outward appearances—but we are even better at being fooled by these same characteristics in others. We are sinful and biased, and since we are so easily deceived by outward appearances, how can we expect to be fair and accurate judges? God alone is righteous, just and all-knowing. Yet, James notes that when we show favoritism toward others, we are in essence trying to sit in the Judge's seat: "Have you not discriminated among yourselves and become judges with evil thoughts?" (Jas. 2:4).

Because showing favoritism is the equivalent of judging, according to James, let's examine the motive behind this spiritual crime. If you show preferential treatment to those who appear to have a lot of money, what is the goal? Perhaps you're hoping they'll say, "Hey, you're a nice person! Let's be best friends. I want to take you out on my yacht, put your kids through college, buy you a Rolex." Friend, that will probably never, ever happen! In fact, James says in verses 6 and 7 that it's the rich who are actually exploiting you, dragging you into court and blaspheming the noble name of Him to whom you belong.

There is only One who is able to elevate and bless you. So, instead of judging others, give up the gavel by handing it to the One to whom it truly belongs. In doing so, you will be free to love and treat everyone you meet equally. This is the fourth most important step in breaking down the walls that divide.

**DOWNLOAD IN PROGRESS**

0%    10%    20%    30%    40%    50%    60%    70%    80%    90%

## Step 5: Put On Your God Goggles

Brian and Jenny both have siblings with special needs. It is one of the many things they have in common that makes them such a lovely match as a married couple. When it came time for them to contemplate starting their own family, they knew their risk of having a child with special needs was much greater than the average couple. However, they decided to have children anyway, because they understood that there is worth and value in every human being.

God blessed them with a healthy baby boy. A few years later, Brian and Jenny tried for a second child and crossed that uncertain road once again. Their second child was also completely and totally healthy.

No matter what their future holds, Brian and Jenny know full well what it means to live with and take care of someone with special needs. They understand the joys, challenges, frustrations and pure wonder and delight these remarkable individuals bring to a family. Brian and Jenny view children as God views them, regardless of whether or not they have special needs.

Their story reminds me of an article by Tania Daniels, a writer for the Charleston, South Carolina, *Missionary Examiner*. She wrote the following:

> When we see people with [God's] eyes, we will look at a child with Down syndrome and recognize the precious spirit within that child . . . a child made in God's image. When we look at someone who is scarred by some sort of tragedy, we will see the beautiful person on the inside. When we see someone from a different race, we will see a potential brother or sister in Christ . . . someone who we may spend eternity with in heaven.[12]

Tania's piece, along with James 2:5-6, uncovers the second to the last step of our app to break down the walls that divide. I like to call it: putting on your "God goggles." James writes, "Has not God chosen those who are poor in the eyes of the world to be rich in faith and to inherit the kingdom he promised those who love him?" (v. 5). And what a stunning revelation into the heart of God! Though we look upon the poor with disdain and have *dishonored* them (see v. 6), James says that our heavenly Father looks upon them with love and compassion and has actually *chosen* them to have an abundance of faith and an inheritance in His kingdom.

If you were to leave your house every day with your most important accessory—the Lord's lens of love—you'd never fail to see those around you as children of God, made in His glorious image (see Gen. 1:26-27) and worthy of His sacrifice on the cross at Calvary (see Mark 10:45). To receive your complimentary pair of God goggles, you simply need to ask Him. Pray and ask the Lord to give you His eyes to see people the way He sees them.

How quickly every divisive barrier would come tumbling down if only we would wake up every morning and ask God to give us His eyes to see all people as He does—regardless of social, economic, racial or ethnic differences! Colossians 3:11-12,14 declares:

> Here there is no Gentile or Jew, circumcised or uncircumcised, barbarian, Scythian, slave or free, but Christ is all, and is in all. Therefore, as God's chosen people, holy and dearly loved, clothe yourselves with compassion, kindness, humility, gentleness and patience. . . . And over all these virtues put on love, which binds them all together in perfect unity.

As you put on your God goggles, and your partiality begins to melt away, may you begin to live out these words in order to break down the walls that divide.

**DOWNLOAD IN PROGRESS**

0%   10%   20%   30%   40%   50%   60%   70%   80%   90%

## Step 6: Regard the Royal Law

The final step in delivering a *coup de grâce* to the walls that divide is found in James 2:8-9: "If you really keep the royal law found in Scripture, 'Love your neighbor as yourself,' you are doing right. But if you show favoritism, you sin and are convicted by the law as lawbreakers." What is James talking about here? In order to understand this critical step of downloading God's app, turn back the pages of your Bible to Matthew 22:34-40, in which Jesus reveals the two most important things we could ever do to please God and bring Him glory.

It's kind of a funny scene when you think about it—like the quiz game show "Win Ben Stein's Money." A couple of political and religious groups fired questions at God's one and only Son, hoping to stump Him, prove their superiority and show Him to be a phony. After Jesus had silenced the challenges of the Sadducees, the Pharisees got together and formulated an inquiry that was sure to be a showstopper. "Teacher," one of them began, feigning reverence, "what is the greatest commandment in the Law?" (Matt. 22:36). This was intended as a trick question, for the Pharisee knew the law well; in fact, Matthew 22:35 tells us that he was "an expert of the law." How could Jesus possibly pick the greatest commandment of the 613 laws found in the Torah?[13]

But calmer than Ben Stein, and quicker than a round of *Double Jeopardy*, Jesus answered quite simply, " 'Love the Lord your God with all your heart and with all your soul and with all your mind.' This is the first and greatest commandment" (v. 37). I love this next part. The Lord, in His divine wisdom and coolness, decided to give His adversaries a bonus answer, just in case any doubt remained that He was indeed the Messiah. "And the second is like it," He continued, " 'Love your neighbor as yourself.' All the Law and the Prophets hang on these two commandments" (vv. 39-40).

Sometimes it may seem like there are a lot of commands and doctrines that we, as Christians, must abide by, but our Savior was so wise and gracious to simplify matters for us. To love God and to love others is the consummation of every last one of the laws in the Old Testament. Thus, James calls this the "royal law." But, as he points out in James 2:9-11, "If you show favoritism, you sin and are convicted by the law as lawbreakers. For whoever keeps the whole law and yet stumbles at just one point is guilty of breaking all of it. For he who said, 'You shall not commit adultery,' also said, 'You shall not murder.' If you do not commit adultery but do commit murder, you have become a lawbreaker."

Favoritism is in direct contradiction to the royal law, because as we learned earlier, it is the equivalent of judging. Instead, James asserts in verse 12 that we should "speak and act as those who are going to be judged by the law that gives freedom." In other words, guard every thought, word and deed as under the scrutiny of Almighty God who will exact judgment upon the world in the last days (see Rev. 22:11-12).

Think about how you drive when a highway patrol car is behind you. You could be the worst driver in the nation, and yet, miraculously, your driving is impeccable during those moments when the eyes of judgment are upon you. But unlike a highway patrolman who relies on physical eyesight and a radar speed gun, God is both omniscient and omnipresent. He sees and knows *everything*! When striving to maintain integrity in our spiritual lives and our interactions with others, remember the truth that you will be called before Christ's judgment seat.

What is the *law that gives freedom* that James is talking about? Simply put, this is the law of grace. When you put your faith in Jesus—believing that He is the Christ, God's one and only Son, whom He raised from the dead—you are set free from the bondage of sin and saved by grace. Romans 8:1-2 confirms this truth: "Therefore, there is now no condemnation for those who are in Christ Jesus, because through Christ Jesus the law of the Spirit who gives life has set you free from the law of sin and death." Please take a moment to open your Bible and read Romans 6:14-15, Galatians 5:4-5 and Ephesians 2:1-10, for more explanation about God's law of grace.

Dear friend, if you abide by this law, you will then extend grace and impartiality to others. Above all, you will extend *love* to others. Since Christ made it abundantly clear that the greatest command is love, let's carefully meditate on and apply its true definition, which is found in 1 Corinthians 13:4-8: "Love is patient, love is kind. It does not envy, it does not boast, it is not proud. It does not dishonor others, it is not self-seeking, it is not easily angered, it keeps no record of wrongs. Love does not delight in evil but rejoices with the truth. It always protects, always trusts, always hopes, always perseveres. Love never fails."

When we learn to love in this manner, we will be able to defeat any bias our hearts might be inclined to entertain. Just take a look at the parable of the Good Samaritan (see Luke 10) and the account of Jesus and the Samaritan woman (see John 4), which are two excellent examples of love's powerful ability to cross racial, ethnic, gender, cultural, religious and social divides. Where love begins, favoritism and prejudice end. So when you choose to *love your neighbor as yourself,* as God commands, you will uphold the royal law found in Scripture and take the final, crucial step in breaking down the invisible walls that divide.

**DOWNLOAD COMPLETE!**

■■■■■■■■■■■■■■■■■■■■■■■■■■■■■■■■■■■■■■■■■■■■■■■■■■■■■■■■

0%    10%    20%    30%    40%    50%    60%    70%    80%    90%

As you've downloaded this particular app, I pray that you have come to find that favoritism has no place among God's people. Thankfully, you and I are given great wisdom in James 2 that has the power to change our heart, transform our church and bless our community. Here's a recap of how we can break down the walls that divide:

- Slather on the oil (repel favoritism with faith).
- Look out for a close cousin to favoritism—prejudice.
- Take a cue from a dog's impartiality.
- Give up the gavel (don't judge based on outward appearances).
- Put on your God goggles (see people as God sees them).
- Regard the royal law of grace (love God and love others).

Dear friend, when I think about what heaven will be like, I'm so glad there are no celebrities, VIPs or MVPs with God. I'm so relieved that I won't have to wait in a long line to sit at the feet of Jesus, while others are promptly escorted to His throne. I'm thankful that I won't have to linger longingly behind the gates of an enormous mansion as the rich and famous enjoy the party inside.

It's awesome to imagine that every seat in heaven will be courtside, and no autographs or photographs will distract me from the glory of our Lord and Savior. You and I, and everyone else present, will be equal. Together we will worship the Almighty God—who alone is worthy of praise and adoration. For eternity we will bask in His great love and impartiality, and every wall that divides us here on earth will be removed forever and ever. Hallelujah!

God Has an App to
# Resuscitate a Dying Faith

## James 2:14-26

One night at a Hard Rock nightclub in Hollywood, Florida, the legendary slugger Jose Canseco was supposed to be fighting in a celebrity boxing match. A former outfielder for the Oakland Athletics and the Texas Rangers, Canseco had been the center of much controversy for steroids use in baseball. His published books *Juiced* and *Vindicated* were among the first to "name names" concerning those who were also taking performance enhancing drugs to compete in major league baseball.

As a way of making money after his baseball career ended, he decided to take up mixed martial arts, and in particular, boxing. But as Canseco's fans showed up to cheer on their hero in the boxing ring at that Hard Rock nightclub, they were met with a scandalous realization. The man in the ring was not Jose Canseco. It was his identical twin brother, Ozzie.

If not for Ozzie's distinctive tattoos, the brothers might have gotten away with it. Ozzie had fooled others before, appearing at book signings for his brother in order to earn cash. This fight was simply another deception.

Disgusted with the bait and switch, the fight promoter immediately took Canseco to court in an attempt to get his money back.[1] I can hardly blame him. After all, when it comes to people, we like to know what we're getting.

If there is one accusation I hear time and again, it is that Christians are hypocrites, and it's difficult to argue against it. At times, it can seem like the church is full of people who are pretending to be someone different or better than they really are. We all have hang-ups and shortcomings, and we all fall short when it comes to following Christ. I know that behind the veneer that many of us have constructed is a faith that wilts with every new disappointment and difficulty.

It makes sense that the word "hypocrite" originally referred to Greek actors—people who would wear masks and pretend to be a character such as a mighty warrior or a noble king. They were impersonators, transforming their voices and faces so that the audience would believe they were someone else. Haven't we all put on masks to disguise ourselves in times of vulnerability? Aren't we all guilty of making certain promises without following through? In all honesty, being hypocritical in word or deed is quite easy to do.

Eighteenth-century British philosopher Edmund Burke once said, "Hypocrisy, of course, can afford to be magnificent in its promises, for never intending to go beyond promise, it costs nothing."[2] While there is a lot of truth to that statement, I would argue that our game of "make-believe" can cost a lot more than we originally thought and turn into something much more harmful if we're not careful. We can become convinced that we need to be "Christian" by label only, rather than living out our faith in a genuine manner.

We can even fool ourselves into concluding that our belief in a certain set of doctrines or our attendance at church every Sunday is all that is required of us as Christians. Of course, as a pastor, I've always been a big proponent of attending church on a regular basis. In fact, I love to tease the seasonal churchgoers at our Easter service by saying, "Merry Christmas to those of you who won't attend until next Easter!" I firmly believe that faithfully gathering together to worship the Lord with other Christians is essential for our spiritual growth (see Heb. 10:24–25). However, we can be fooled into practicing "parking lot Christianity," a faith that we leave in the church parking lot on Sunday afternoon until we come back the next Sunday morning to retrieve it.

If we fail to take our faith beyond the superficial, it can waver over time and slowly degenerate into a monotonous ritual. Consider the haunting words of Dietrich Bonhoeffer, a German pastor, theologian and martyr at the age of 39: "The Christian life comes to mean nothing more than living in the world and as the world, in being no different from the world . . . The upshot of it all is that my only duty as a Christian is to leave the world for an hour or so on a Sunday morning and go to church and be assured that all my sins are forgiven. I need no longer try to follow Christ, for cheap grace . . . has freed me from that."[3]

Bonhoeffer's words sting a little, don't they? Because they are painfully true. When we simply go through the motions of Christian "appearances," we become no different from the rest of the world, for we live the same lives, speak the same words, listen to the same music and treat people in the same manner that nonbelievers do.

Jesus uniquely calls us the "salt of the earth" and the "light of the world" (Matt. 5:13-14). In order to be salt and light, you and I must do more than simply show up at church for an hour or so every weekend. Instead, it's imperative that we passionately take hold of Jesus' instructions to share the gospel with those around us, emulating Christ in all we do and say.

During His three-year ministry on earth, Jesus healed the sick; He spent time with those living on the bottom rung of society; He taught His followers how to exchange their anger and lust for holiness; He demonstrated love for all people regardless of their actions toward Him. He commanded His disciples to imitate the lifestyle He represented, and together they changed the world.

When you first came to Jesus, you were captivated by His love, grace and the salvation He freely offered through His death on Calvary's cross. Wasn't it an exhilarating experience to finally commit your life to the Lord, allowing Him to change you from the inside out? Didn't you see yourself on a path to become a strong prayer warrior and a diligent studier of the Scriptures? And didn't every new command and teaching you learned from God's Word fine-tune your daily lifestyle so that it mirrored, more and more, the lifestyle of Jesus? You were at the top of the world, a saved and sanctified disciple of Jesus Christ, ready to defeat every spiritual stronghold, in His name.

But for one reason or another, the freshness of your newfound faith dissipated. Your Christian walk became an uphill battle. The joy you once possessed was exchanged for skepticism. You may have been forced to endure a difficult trial and were unable to explain why God didn't intervene. Perhaps God met your prayers with answers you didn't understand or appreciate. Or maybe the Christian life didn't line up with what you expected it to be, and then your enthusiasm began to turn stale like a sad slice of sourdough bread. Have any or all of these reasons, together with the tiring shuffle of everyday life, caused your heart to become calloused to the initial impact of meeting Christ?

Someone once said, "The problem with life is that it is so *daily*." What this means for the believer is that we can easily get caught up in the doldrums of the rigmarole. This isn't an uncommon problem.

All of us, at some time, have fallen in love or discovered a new thrill, only to watch that initial passion slowly wane to indifference. For instance, have you ever bought a piano or a guitar? If so, it's very likely that you fully intended to master that musical instrument, logging in numerous hours of rehearsal. But after a while, the practice became tedious and mind numbing. You may have felt as if you weren't getting any better and that all of your practice was just wasted time. Ultimately, you took that instrument to the attic and banished it to a life of dust and rust.

The same digression that sometimes occurs with our passion for a hobby can also take place in our relationships with one another. As any married couple will tell you, the first months of marriage are easy. Each argument can be easily resolved and every difficulty effortlessly defused. Once that honeymoon period is over, however, the hard work to establish a lasting marriage begins.

For many of us, the honeymoon period of our Christian walk has ended and our fervent devotion to God has been cast aside. The church of Ephesus was reminded by Jesus in Revelation 2:4-5 that they had forsaken their first love and had fallen from great heights. Jesus issues this challenge to today's Church as well—to believers who have forsaken their first love and let their spiritual lives plummet.

Dear friend, if your zeal for the gospel has grown stale, if you're weary of practicing a superficial faith or you have left your first love, your faith may be in desperate need of resuscitation. But here's a positive prognosis: By downloading God's app to resuscitate a dying faith, you can obtain an authentic and vibrant Christian walk once again! Your commitment to the Lord will be infused with new life, vigor and effervescent joy as you examine the truth found in James 2:14-26.

Before we begin, take note that it isn't a simple drag-and-drop instant download, like acquiring a flashlight app or Angry Birds. Think Windows 7 or Mac OS X—an entire operating system that affects the way *everything* works. This is an application that has the power to change how we live, bolstering our sincerity and effectiveness for the kingdom of God. So let's get started!

### BEGIN DOWNLOAD

0%    10%    20%    30%    40%    50%    60%    70%    80%    90%

## Step 1: Get Back to Basics

It has been said that a real chess pro is able to foresee the entire progression of a game at the first move. While the average chess player usually just moves pieces around, hoping to eventually win, the professionals understand the importance of the first move. They know it could be the difference between winning and losing.

Likewise, the first move to resuscitate a dying faith is critical. It involves determining whether our faith was alive in the first place. The focus of our text, James 2:14-26, is centered on "faith" and "deeds," and on how the two work in tandem to produce a fruitful Christian life. Before we can address the subject of "deeds," we must go back to Christianity 101 and understand the meaning of "faith."

Typically, when Christians use the word "faith," they are referring to doctrine. The phrase "our faith" stands for "what we believe" or "the basic principles of Christianity." This set of beliefs, found in the Word of God, are the very core of a mature and healthy Christian walk. Inherent in each doctrine is something cognitive, something you can know and express with words and ideas. For example, we believe that Jesus Christ was virgin-born, sinless, died on the cross for the world's sins, was raised from the dead on the third day and is coming again (see Matt. 1:18; Heb. 4:15; 1 Cor.15:3-4; John 14:3). We also believe that God is one, and yet He exists in three persons: the Father, the Son and the Holy Spirit. We believe that the Bible is the Word of God, which He inspired and created for our instruction and training for righteousness (see Tim. 3:16-17). We believe these statements are true, and together, they represent what we have called "faith."

Neglecting these foundational elements of doctrine would be disastrous. It would be like having muscles and ligaments without a skeleton—the entire body would droop and sag. That's not a pretty picture, is it? For this reason, it's crucial that we recognize that our beliefs are what build us up, causing us to stand tall and strong in our Christian walk.

But to merely think about "faith" as "doctrine" would miss the wider scope. The emphasis for faith is not *what* we believe; it's *in whom* we believe. The *object* of our faith is the important part. Anyone can place his or her faith in a rock or a tree or a cloud, but in the end, that type of faith would be worthless. I've actually heard of a religious group called the Pastafarians who worship a being called the Flying Spaghetti Monster.[4] Unfortunately for them, their faith in their "god" is pointless, because they've placed it in "someone" who cannot help them. It wouldn't matter if these Pastafarians invented an elaborate web of doctrines, or even believed in them, because they have chosen the wrong recipient for their faith. As a result, they have no assurance that their faith will be answered.

Paul writes in Romans 3:22, "Righteousness is given through faith in Jesus Christ to all who believe." The key phrase in this verse is "in Jesus Christ." God's righteousness is birthed in us when we put our faith in the person of Jesus Christ. If we have not placed our faith in Jesus, then everything we believe about Jesus is futile.

Another way to translate the word "faith" would be "trust" or "allegiance."[5] When we place our faith in Jesus, we are placing our complete trust in Him. As a patriot pledges allegiance to his country, to have faith in Jesus means that we pledge our allegiance to Him. If you make this pledge, then it requires that you hand over everything in your life to His will. To hold back any part of your life—your job, your friendships, your marriage, your free time— simply reveals that you haven't fully committed your trust to Jesus, the only one who can truly save you from your sins.

So the question of all questions is: *Have you placed your faith and trust in Jesus Christ?* If you cannot answer this question in the affirmative, if you do not get back to basics by renewing your trust in Jesus, the Son of the Living God, then you'll never receive that first vital breath of air that is essential to resuscitating a dying faith. Like a knight vowing his devotion to a king, when you place your faith in Jesus Christ, you are proclaiming that He is the King of all kings and the Lord of all lords. And if you can sincerely make that pledge, renewing your trust in the Savior and surrendering every aspect of your life to Him, then your once-wilting faith will receive a vital breath of new life!

**DOWNLOAD IN PROGRESS**

0%    10%    20%    30%    40%    50%    60%    70%    80%    90%

## Step 2: Balance the Teeter-Totter

James begins our text in 2:14 by asking one of the most crucial questions we face as followers of Jesus: "What good is it, my brothers and sisters, if someone claims to have faith but has no deeds? Can such faith save them?" To answer this question, our author sets up a hypothetical situation for us to consider: Suppose we happen upon a person who is without clothing or daily food. In James's day, this wasn't uncommon, as many people living at that time were peasants or workers who lived hand-to-mouth every day. A local patron—a person of extravagant wealth who could afford to employ local workers in his or her fields, barns or house—supported these peasants.[6] Now, suppose we happen upon a peasant who has no patron. No one is taking care of him. He has literally nothing to wear, and he hasn't received his daily ration of food. He has nothing.

If we say to this person, "Go, I wish you well. Good luck. God bless. Keep warm and well fed," and yet do nothing to feed or clothe him, James asks, "What good is it?" In other words, "Who are we kidding?" Quite literally, this person has nothing—no clothing, no food and most likely no shelter. He doesn't even have the bare necessities, and if a word of empty encouragement is all a follower of Jesus can offer, then we have missed the mark; we have not properly shown the love and provision that Jesus has shown to us. We have not represented Christ to our world.

What's worse is that James indicates that this type of neglect is not a one-time occurrence; this is something that is happening over and over.[7] When believers make a habit of ignoring those without food and clothing, it goes beyond a single lapse of judgment. We're talking about a continual attitude of withholding blessing from those who have nothing.

This behavior is so strange, because helping those who are destitute has always been a cornerstone of the Christian faith. Jesus' instructions to the rich young ruler who claimed to have obeyed all of the Ten Commandments was this: "Go, sell everything you have and *give to the poor*, and you will have treasure in heaven" (Mark 10:21, emphasis added). The Lord even went so far as to say that providing food, drink or clothing to those who have none, and visiting the sick and the imprisoned—doing good for the "least of these"—is the equivalent of doing good for Him (see Matt. 25:34-40).

So, when James writes that these hypothetical Christians are continually passing by the poor, whom God deeply cares about, it is a prime example of how having *faith* in God's provision for the poor is useless if it is not accompanied with *action* by blessing those who have nothing. It is not enough to believe and hope that God will take care of the impoverished; we must remember that God will indeed take care of them through us—through our generous, selfless and compassionate deeds!

James takes this idea a step further: "Faith by itself, if it is not accompanied by action, is dead" (2:17). Have you ever seen a child sitting alone on a teeter-totter at the park, trying with all his or her might to push against the ground and get the teeter-totter to move? It doesn't take the child long to realize this contraption needs two people to function. In the same way, when we attempt to live by faith alone, our Christian walk goes nowhere—without deeds there is nothing on the other end, balancing the teeter-totter and enabling us to move.

Just like you cannot have Lucy without Ricky, Mulder without Scully, Barnes without Noble, Kermit without Miss Piggy, Abbott without Costello, you cannot have faith without works. As the late Christian songwriter Rich Mullins penned in his song "Screen Door": "Faith without works is like a song you can't sing. It's about as useless as a screen door on a submarine."[8]

As we continue to download God's app to resuscitate a dying faith, we must possess the proper balance of faith and deeds working together. This critical passage in James shows us that believing the "right things" isn't enough. Our faith is proven when we put it into action by serving God and others in our everyday lives.

**DOWNLOAD IN PROGRESS**

0%  10%  20%  30%  40%  50%  60%  70%  80%  90%

## Step 3: Shudder at the Possibilities

When James wrote in 2:19, "You believe that there is one God. Good! Even the demons believe that—and shudder," his readers who were Jewish Christians would have instantly recognized that he was intentionally referring to the most important verse in the Old Testament. He was talking about the Shema,[9] which is found in Deuteronomy 6:4-5 and says, "Hear, O Israel: The LORD our God, the LORD is one. Love the LORD your God with all your heart and with all your soul and with all your strength."

Every Israelite knew the Shema by heart. In fact, they quoted it every day. These words represented for them—and for us—a declaration of devotion to the kingdom of God. It was their anthem, their pledge. Some rabbis even believed that if you spoke the Shema as slowly as possible, it would lengthen your life.[10] When we downloaded God's app to break down the walls that divide, in the previous chapter, we discussed how Jesus Himself pointed to Deuteronomy 6:4 as the greatest commandment in God's Word. Thus, we are talking about the very center of our faith, that God—existing in the persons of the Father, Son and Holy Spirit—is one.

But even the demons believe that God is one, James argues, and because of this belief they shudder, shake and tremble in fear. In this way, and in this way only, should we be like the demons. The fact that they shudder at God's oneness is proof that His very nature is something to be feared. After all, we're talking about the one who has the capacity to flood the entire earth; who can send plagues of frogs, locusts and flies; who can split formidable seas down the middle and set mountains on fire. We're talking about the one who has the ability to raise men from the dead; who created the entire universe and can reduce it to dust in an instant if He wanted to. The demons are quivering in fear for a reason, and to some extent, so should we. Please allow me to explain.

When the prophet Isaiah had a vision of the Lord seated on a throne (see Isa. 6), the train of God's robe filled the whole temple with glory. Peculiar-looking six-winged angels flew around and proclaimed God's holiness, causing the doorposts and thresholds to shake and the temple to fill with smoke. But the only words Isaiah could muster were, "Woe to me! . . . I am ruined! For I am a man of unclean lips, and I live among a people of unclean lips, and my eyes have seen the King, the LORD Almighty" (6:5). In the terrifying presence of the Lord, all Isaiah could think about was his own sinfulness and how holy, great and majestic is the Creator of the universe!

Like Isaiah, fear is our initial response to God's holiness—falling on our faces and shrinking from His light, afraid that we will be destroyed for our sinfulness. The Lord, however, does not wish to destroy us. He loves us, and He demonstrated His heart and compassion toward us by sending His one and only Son to die on our behalf so that we could spend eternity with Him.

We should not fear the Lord in the ways that demons do. They quiver in fear because they know that everlasting punishment awaits them for disobeying God; but if we live lives aimed at pleasing our Father in heaven, then we do not fear this punishment. When the Bible tells us to fear the Lord,[11] it doesn't mean that we should cower in the corner and wait for God to roll through with righteous vengeance. For the believer, fearing the Lord is having a holy respect for a holy God. We do not shudder with dread. Instead, we shudder at the possibilities of God's greatness in our lives and marvel at the lengths to which He can display His love for us.

So you see, as you attempt to revitalize your faith, the third step is to realize that faith and action must be rooted in a reverent fear of the Father. He alone is worthy of your awe and your praise; and when you recognize His incomparably glorious nature, you can't help but tremble in His presence.

**DOWNLOAD IN PROGRESS**

0%   10%   20%   30%   40%   50%   60%   70%   80%   90%

## Step 4: Grab Your Toolbox

On any given weekend at our church, we have many first-time visitors, and with approximately 10,000 other attendees, I know it would be easy for these newcomers to feel lost or unsure about where they might fit in. Among the other ways we help new people feel connected, there's an illustration that I like to use sometimes when I'm speaking.

"How many of you are visiting our church for the very first time today?" I ask. "Please raise your hands."

Inevitably, dozens of hands will go up, so I choose one person to come up on stage with me. I instruct this person to cross his arms in front of his chest like he's about to perform a Russian dance, and then I tell him to say aloud for the whole congregation to hear, "I wonder what this church can offer me?"

Then I tell everyone in the congregation to cross their arms like the man on stage, and I direct them to say in unison, "I wonder what this man can offer us?"

Some folks in the audience will immediately pick up on the purpose of the exercise, but others will be noticeably confused, so I continue by reversing this visual illustration. I ask the man on stage to stretch out his arms toward the church, and I tell him to say, "I wonder what gifts and talents I have to serve these beautiful people?"

Next, I instruct everyone in the crowd to stretch out their arms toward the newcomer. A sea of arms unfold and reach out toward the man on stage like fans at a rock concert. With one voice the crowd says to the man, "I wonder what gifts and talents we have to serve this handsome man?"

Can you imagine an entire auditorium of people with their arms outstretched toward you, wondering out loud how they could best serve you? I've seen some newcomers visibly moved by this display of service. And they all leave thinking the same thing: *This is no ordinary church!*

Whenever people walk into church expecting to be served, no one gets served. But if these same people enter the church willing to serve others, then everyone will be helped and blessed. If you want to resuscitate a dying faith, begin by asking the question, "What can I possibly do to serve others in my church and in my community?" Thus, this step requires you to pull out your figurative toolbox and determine how you can help others right now.

We all have skills and abilities that could be used in service to others. Whether you're a whiz with computers, a bookworm, an expert dishwasher or an inspiring sports coach, your gifts are precious to God, no matter how insignificant you might think they are. You'd actually be surprised at the skill sets that can be used to build God's Church. For instance, my friend Tom designs mobile phone applications. He's a genius at it, too, having designed apps for Oprah Winfrey, the NFL and other corporate titans.

One day, while Tom was in Paris, France, and happened to be listening online to one of my sermons on giftedness and using one's skills to further God's kingdom, a life-changing idea came to him: He decided to use his expertise to create a mobile phone application called "CallOnJesus," which would allow anyone in the world to download videos of my sermons as well as the sermons of many other respected preachers in the U.S. He also added a couple of bonus features, such as my 365-day devotional titled *Romancing Royalty* and a "Bible in a Year" reader.[12]

Like Tom, you have to decide what gifts and talents God has placed inside of you and determine to use those skills to further His Kingdom. You may not be able to create something as elaborate as a mobile phone application, but that certainly doesn't mean your abilities aren't needed. For example, you might be one of those people who will immediately pick up another book as soon as you've finished this one. Your friends may even accuse you of reading too much, but they may not realize that your compulsion for devouring literature and magazine articles can be extremely useful in your church. You can record stories, illustrations or quotes that you find particularly engaging and offer them to the preachers and teachers in your congregation. (I'm always looking for interesting material to share in my sermons!) Just because you're not up front and teaching doesn't mean that your knowledge isn't valuable. Your hobby literally could bless others!

If you delight in taking care of preschoolers, then put this skill to use by volunteering in the children's ministry department for your local church. Perhaps you are excellent at planning events or coordinating programs; if so, many ministries are always looking for highly organized people to give of their time. You might be handy around the house, fixing leaks and creaks and making home improvements. Offer your services free of charge to those in your church community and in your neighborhood. Or maybe you are obsessed with "green" initiatives; begin a recycling ministry and use the proceeds for ministries like Generosity Water that set up sources of clean drinking water for third-world countries.

Take some time right now and open up your figurative "toolbox," compiling a list of your skills and abilities. Write down as many as possible, no matter how silly or ridiculous they seem.

When you're finished, review the list and ask yourself, "How can I put these to work in my church and in my community?" After you prayerfully evaluate what you can do to bless others, you will be amazed at how quickly new life will flow into your faith.

**DOWNLOAD IN PROGRESS**

0%    10%    20%    30%    40%    50%    60%    70%    80%    90%

## Step 5: Show, Don't Tell

During World War II, Corrie ten Boom and her sister Betsie were taken to a concentration camp called Ravensbruck. They were being punished for housing Jews in the Netherlands. While at Ravensbruck, they suffered terrible abuse by the guards and the conditions of the camp, and Betsie finally died from mistreatment.

After the Nazis were defeated, Corrie was released and went about helping to heal her homeland from the devastation caused by the war. Her story became famous, and she was asked to speak all over Europe and America. It was after a church service in Munich that she recognized one of the Ravensbruck guards who had been responsible for her sister's death. The former guard strode right up to her and thanked her heartily. Her message, after all, was about how Jesus' death forgives us of our sins, a message that hit home with him.

It was clear that he did not recognize her from the camp, because the man held out his hand to shake hers. At first, she could not. Anger and vengeful thoughts consumed her so much that her hand stayed frozen at her side. She understood that Jesus had died for this man, but it was much too difficult for her to forgive him. She prayed, "Jesus, I cannot forgive him. Give me Your forgiveness." As she took his hand, it was as if a current passed from her to him, and her feelings of anger and revenge melted away into love and compassion for this person. The forgiveness of Jesus Christ reached right through her as she reached out to this man.[13]

I love this story because it shows that we can't simply talk about Christ's forgiveness to others; we have to show it. In fact, the credo of every novelist and film director is "Show, don't tell," because a story is not very interesting if we are told what happened or what should happen. Instead, it's better to let the story show how a journey unfolds. This is the same with Scripture and theology. It's no accident that about 40 percent of the Old Testament and 60 percent of the New Testament is composed of historical narrative.[14] Sometimes, if you want to make your point, you need to paint a picture in living color.

James is no stranger to the "show, don't tell" rule. He writes in James 2:18, "Show me your faith without deeds, and I will show you my faith by my deeds." This is the path we must travel in order to bolster our faith with action. It happens when we figure out what we believe and then put that belief into action. Corrie ten Boom believed that God had forgiven her of her sins, but her belief would mean nothing if she couldn't display that same forgiveness to someone else, even if that person was partially responsible for the death of her own sister.

The very moment we decide that our Christian faith is a private matter between God and us is exactly the moment we've lost our faith. If Corrie could not extend forgiveness to the former Nazi soldier, then how could she believe that God would extend that same forgiveness to her? In the same way, our Father expects us, as His children, to show precisely what we believe in real and practical ways so that the world may understand His love.

Do you believe that God brings comfort to those who are suffering? If so, partner with God in the ministry of comfort, visiting those who are afflicted in hospitals and nursing homes. Do you believe that God cares about the poor and dispossessed? If so, reach out to the impoverished in your community by distributing food, clothing and blankets. If we don't *show* others what we believe by what we do, we're stopping short of what God desires for us. Instead, the words of the apostle John should be our anthem: "Dear children, let us not love with words or speech but with actions and in truth" (1 John 3:18).

Imagine if Dr. Martin Luther King—after all of his preaching and conviction about racial equality in America—had done nothing to make it a reality. Suppose that he never made phone calls to or-ganize restaurant sit-ins or bus boycotts. What if he never put him-self in harm's way or went to prison for civil disobedience? Maybe he decided that marching to Washington, DC, wasn't such a good idea after all. Imagine if his "I Have a Dream" speech was really just a dream, never a vision that would become a reality someday. What if they were just words?

What if Desmond Tutu had never fought against apartheid in South Africa? What if Jim Elliot had never flown to Ecuador to evangelize the Auca Indians? What if Hudson Taylor had never sailed to China to share the gospel with the Chinese? What if Mother Teresa had never traveled to Calcutta to care for the poor, the sick and the orphaned?

What if Moses had never returned to Egypt to free the Israelites, or if David had never slung his stone against the giant Goliath? What if Ezra and Nehemiah had not led the Israelites back to their country from captivity? What if Peter had not dropped his nets to follow Jesus? What if Matthew had not left his tax booth? What if Paul had ignored the blinding light on the road to Damascus?

What if Jesus had not died on the cross? What if He had not risen again? What if He had never come at all?

What if our intentions were only that, intentions, but never ac-tion? Dear friend, we must show the world around us what we be-lieve in our hearts to be true. And when we "show, don't tell," we will be one step closer to bringing our faith back to life completely.

**DOWNLOAD IN PROGRESS**

■■■■■■■■■■■■■■■■■■■■■■■■■■■■■■■■■■■■■■■■■■■■■■■■■■■■■■■■■■■■■■■■■□□

0%    10%    20%    30%    40%    50%    60%    70%    80%    90%

## Step 6: Get Your Head in the Clouds

The final step in God's app to resuscitate a dying faith is to re-member that you're not alone in this struggle toward achieving a faithful walk with the Lord. There have been myriads of believers who have gone before you and are cheering you on toward the fin-ish line, as well as Christians who are alive today and working together to accomplish God's purposes. The Christian life does not require us to reinvent the proverbial wheel, especially since we have so much to learn from those who have followed God with a steadfast faith.

In James 2:21-26, our author presents two characters whose lives model an active and vibrant faith. James first presents Abraham, the "father" of the Israelites, whose faith defies rationality. This man trusted God to the extent that he left his family and his homeland of 75 years and ventured out into unknown territory simply because God commanded it. He wholeheartedly believed God when God promised him a child, even though Abraham and his wife, Sarah, were already quite old. When God came through on His promise, Abraham believed that God intended him only good when He asked Abraham to sacrifice that very son to Him. With the knife inches from his son Isaac's throat, Abraham was prepared to show his trust in God's sovereignty. And God answered him by sparing his son (see Gen. 22:1-19).

Abraham *showed* his faith in God. Abraham's faith wasn't a mere contract that he could abandon as soon as he got what he wanted. Even when God demanded what Abraham cherished the most, his son, he did not shrink away from his responsibility. He acted out his belief in God's providence.

James also tells the story of Rahab, the prostitute of Jericho. After the Israelites emerged from wandering in the desert for 40 years, they came to take possession of the Promised Land, but a city called Jericho stood in their way. So Joshua sent two spies to this city in order to discern their military strength. The spies stayed in the house of this Rahab, the town prostitute (see Josh. 2).

Word soon reached the king of Jericho that Israelite spies were hiding at Rahab's house, so he dispatched soldiers to kill them; but before they arrived, Rahab hid the two spies under stalks of flax on her roof. When the soldiers interrogated her, she didn't waver under the pressure, telling them that the spies had already left.

When the soldiers had gone, she called the spies back inside and encouraged them to invade Jericho, because obviously the people of Jericho were frightened of the Israelites. News of the power of the Lord had reached from Egypt across the wilderness to Jericho, and Rahab had decided that she would place her trust in this God instead of the false gods of the Canaanites. Therefore, she acted on this faith, siding with the armies of Israel—and with the God who protected them—by helping the two Israelite spies to escape.

These stories of Abraham and Rahab aren't the only ones. Just read what is called "the faith chapter," Hebrews 11, for an inspiring documentation of those who acted out on their faith. We haven't even covered the stuttering Moses who led a nation to freedom or the aging Noah who built a massive boat to weather a flood, though it had never rained before. We haven't even spoken of faithful heroes like Gideon or Samson or David or Daniel. But what is so shocking is that these heroes "were all commended for their faith, yet none of them received what had been promised, since God had planned something better for us so that only together with us would they be made perfect" (Heb. 11:39-40). Did you get the full weight of that? They are *waiting for us* before they can receive God's full promise of perfection. When Jesus returns for us, these saints who have gone before us will finally see the consummation and perfection of all things.

None of the Old Testament heroes of faith received the grace of Jesus Christ during their natural lifetime. Yet all of them looked forward to a time when sins would be forgiven, when God would live together with His creation, when death would finally be defeated. They believed in God and in His promises, and they acted accordingly.

As believers, you and I file into a long line of heroes who displayed their faith in God even to the point of losing their lives. We're not the first Jesus-followers on the block, nor are we the first people in the world to show God's love. God's mission to save the world from sin has been going on for millennia, and even now we're not acting alone to accomplish that goal.

The author of Hebrews, after writing about these warriors of the faith, begins Hebrews 12 in this way: "Therefore, since we are surrounded by such a great cloud of witnesses, let us throw off everything that hinders and the sin that so easily entangles, and let us run with perseverance the race marked out for us" (v. 1). In a manner of speaking, the Christian life is a race, one that requires great endurance and considerable focus. But this race isn't an individual sprint. It's a relay race. Like athletes passing a baton, or the Olympic runners passing the torch, Jesus' command to His apostles to make disciples has been progressing across centuries through faithful believers. And even now they cheer for us on a metaphorical cloud in the sky, looking down on us as we run our race with confidence.

Likewise, there are Christians here and now who are striving to deliver the gospel to those who are in desperate need of a Savior, running the same race we're running. Therefore, let us work together—network and collaborate—in our ministerial efforts. Together we'll be able to accomplish much more than if we worked alone.

Knowing that you are not alone in the race of faith is the final step for this application download. An entire cloud of believers has gone before you—in addition to faithful believers around the world who are working diligently to share the good news of God's grace with every nation, tribe, language and people. So get your head in the clouds by joining a global initiative that began at creation and stretches all the way to the end of time, and watch your faith come alive.

### DOWNLOAD COMPLETE!

In this chapter, we've discovered these six steps toward downloading God's app for resuscitating a dying faith:

- Realize that faith begins with what we believe about God and His Word. Once we know the fundamentals, we can truly begin to restore a withering faith.
- Balance the importance of faith and action, because you can't have one without the other.
- Maintain a holy reverence for a holy God, remembering that demons tremble in the face of God's sovereignty and power—because while they believe, they do not obey.

- Evaluate the contents of your spiritual toolbox, using your gifts and talents to bless others.
- Begin to show your beliefs through your actions. Display God's love in this world so that others might see it and believe.
- Remember that we are not alone in this struggle. Our faith is bolstered by the heroes of faith who have gone before, and by today's Church that works diligently to save the lost.

If you have been experiencing a faltering faith or a lackluster walk with Christ, I pray that by downloading this critical app, you have rekindled the love and passion you had when you first met Jesus. Sometimes, as believers, we can allow our faith to drown in a sea of cares and worries that distract us from our goal and mission for the kingdom of God. It is during those times that we need a Lifesaver to come and breathe new life into our spiritual lungs. That Lifesaver is Jesus, and He declares, "I have come that they may have life, and have it to the full" (John 10:10).

# God Has an App to
# Curb Your Profanity

## James 3:1-12

Years ago, I took my two oldest children to a Los Angeles Dodgers baseball game, which is usually a fun and satisfying experience—nine innings of quality baseball, viewing America's favorite pastime with my kids, while consuming overly priced peanuts, a soda and a Dodger Dog, of course. But on this particular night, a group of young men sat directly behind us, and with each beer they consumed their language became more offensive. Whether it was a response to a good call, a bad call or a cute girl walking by, they found any and every reason to use every expletive in the book. Frustrated, I finally turned around and said sternly, "Hey, I'm trying to enjoy this game, so please stop using those swear words around me and my children."

They snickered as I turned back around, but I certainly didn't mind playing the "uptight father" role—the last thing I wanted was my young children to hear such foul language and think it was "cool." As you can imagine, it was only a matter of minutes before the cursing continued. I grew more and more upset and began to wonder whether or not I should get security involved. But the sad reality is that whether I am at a Dodger game (or almost anywhere else, for that matter), ultimately I will be unable to protect my children's ears, much less my own, from this kind of language. No matter where one goes, sinful speech abounds.

Just recently at a popular fitness chain near my house, I was participating in my favorite cardio workout—the "cycling class" in which you ride a stationary bike for about an hour at various speeds and in-clines. I try to take the cycling class at least two or three times a week, even though I feel like a giant hamster on a wheel, because I always feel energized afterward. During this particular session, I was ready to put the pedal to the metal when the instructor pressed "play" on the stereo system, suddenly unleashing songs that were filled with derogatory language. I was shocked. After all, this was a public place! Why should I have to pay a gym fee to listen to this kind of music?

We live in a culture where foul language has become the norm. I'm not just talking about cursing; I'm talking about a society that uses demeaning and abusive language in everyday conversation, that watches and engages in an endless news cycle of destructive gossip and proclaims a general attitude of cynicism that makes comedic hay out of others' misfortunes. What's worse, I don't just hear this type of language in the media; I'm hearing it from people who call themselves Christians.

Have we not realized that the gift of language was created with the best of God's intentions? With our words we are able to paint beautiful pictures, tell colorful stories, build others up, articulate our opinions, construct persuasive arguments and express love. However, as with so many other things, we have misused and abused the Lord's perfect creation. Foul and perverse words sneak into our everyday vocabulary. When we should be speaking only truth and edification, instead we spew deceit and derision. In place of words of encourage-ment, hate, pride and criticism drip from haughty lips. Expressions of kindness and acceptance are exchanged for racial slurs that divide and demean. Gossip is exhaled into our spiritual environment, fur-thering its pollution. We have even been so audacious as to take the holy name of the *Lord God Almighty*, and use it as a curse word.

How have we wandered so far from righteousness?

The first thing we must get through our heads is the severity of this problem. To many of us, foul language doesn't seem like a big deal. We hear it everywhere—in movies, on television, in the songs on the radio, from our friends, siblings and even from our own par-ents. I read a cute story about a little girl who tattled on her daddy, saying how upset her mommy gets when he uses his "bowling words" in the house. While the innocence of her statement may bring a smile to your face, it nonetheless calls attention to a sobering truth: We have taken our sinful speech, fluffed it up and called it "bowling words." We justify that foul words aren't a big deal if we're in the midst of a fierce competition; we rationalize that gossip is not a big deal if spoken confidentially to our girlfriends, or that off-color humor isn't a big deal when we're with the guys.

Jesus Himself made it clear that the words we speak carry extreme importance. We can't miss this crucial passage of Scripture in which He gives this stern admonition: "But I tell you that everyone will have to give account on the day of judgment for every empty word they have spoken. For by your words you will be acquitted, and by your words you will be condemned" (Matt. 12:36-37).

Jesus wished to impress upon His followers the gravity of what we say. Our speech not only affects our present, but also our eternity, so we cannot afford to allow our speech to go unchecked. If you're not yet convinced, let me give you four concise reasons why you ought to turn from coarse language.

## Coarse Language Turns Your Heart Away from God

Two monks in a monastery were locked in a debate; each was convinced that he was more humble than the other. Unable to solve this dispute, they decided to put their humility to the test. Whenever they spoke to one another, they would use the most degrading speech possible to get the other to stumble. For weeks they went on like this, persistently cutting each other down with coarse remarks in an attempt to enflame the other's pride. However, as their speech became more and more disgusting, their lifestyle followed suit. Soon, both of them decided to leave the monastery and live a life of depravity.

This story illustrates the simple truth that no matter who you are or how holy or humble you think you might be, the more you listen to and use foul language, the more you can be enticed to fall away. In the book of Psalms, David wrote: "The mouth of the righteous utters wisdom, and their tongues speak what is just. The law of his God is in their hearts; their feet do not slip" (Ps. 37:30-31). For David, speech was directly correlated to the heart. A mouth that utters wisdom and justice is connected to a heart devoted to God; but a mouth spouting foolishness and offense is connected to a heart separated from Him.

## Coarse Language Misrepresents Christ

Christian comedian Jim Labriola knows this truth all too well. Widely recognized as the deliveryman on the sitcom *Home Improvement,* Jim's early comedic career was built on R-rated humor. For him, comedy was about mixing curse words with innuendo in creative combinations to get a laugh from the audience. But after Jim decided to give his life to Christ, he realized that he would have to change a significant part of his comedy routine in order to be true to his faith. He just couldn't escape Ephesians 5:4, which says, "Nor should there be obscenity, foolish talk or coarse joking, which are out of place, but rather thanksgiving."

He decided to take a break from comedy for three years in order to write new material for a completely different act. Now he is a well-received Christian comic, entertaining audiences with clean jokes. Not only did believers start reacting positively to his new stand-up act, but secular audiences also appreciated his family-friendly material.

In his own words, Jim says, "Always remember that you are representing God, because people are always looking at you."[1] We represent Christ with our speech. As believers, when people hear us speaking they ought to hear Christ speaking through us. But if we pollute our mouths with foul language, we seriously injure Christ's reputation.

## Coarse Language Injures Your Integrity

In verse 1 of chapter 3, James acknowledged how difficult it is to set an example to others with our speech by indicating that many of us are not even suited to take on leadership or teaching roles. Why? Because we will be held to a more stringent accountability for our every word and deed. I can certainly testify to this! One of the greatest challenges I face in leading a church is that everything I say will be scrutinized. I am not complaining; this simply comes with the territory of my vocation as a pastor. That being said, you can imagine how important it has been in my life to maintain purity of speech. A single moment of expressed frustration on the golf course with my buddies can nullify my ministry from the pulpit.

I received a call on my cell phone from an unknown number. I answered and quickly realized that the person had "pocket dialed" me—his phone had called mine unintentionally. The man did not know I had picked up the call, and I overheard part of his conversation, which was filled with curse word after curse word. Though the caller's name was not identified on my screen, I recognized his voice because he had recently preached at my church! I was shocked, and I couldn't in good conscience invite the man to speak at my church again.

Why? Because this kind of language destroys one's credibility! Having heard this man use such foul language, how could I possibly respect his preaching? Imagine if you were entering a church and were heartily welcomed to the Sunday service by the greeters standing at the door, only to hear them gossiping about others in the church after you passed by? Would you feel like you had just walked into a sincere and positive environment? Or what if the children's ministry volunteers were using swear words in their conversation? Would you want to leave your kids in their care? I certainly wouldn't!

You see, this kind of language damages our integrity as Christian servants and erases Christ's stamp on our work. But if we put away this kind of language, then our integrity remains intact and people will more readily trust us as servants of Christ.

## Coarse Language Damages Your Relationships

If you've ever heard the old childhood taunt "Sticks and stones may break my bones, but words will never hurt me," you also know that it's completely untrue. Harshly spoken words can hurt for a lifetime, and relationships are hardly exempt from their devastating effect.

I've sat in on marriage counseling sessions where the spouses absolutely obliterated each other with their words. I wondered, *If they could just change the way they spoke to each other, could their relationship be mended?* If we seasoned our conversation with grace, as Colossians 4:6 teaches us to do, I am convinced that sour relationships would quickly freshen. We would see an immediate drop in broken relationships and divorce, because instead of seeking to hurt with our words, we would be dedicated to building others up.

I often tell soon-to-be-married couples that every hurtful word is like laying down a single brick. Over time, the bricks begin to pile up until a wall stands between the couple—much too towering to surmount. Whether in the context of a marriage, a family relationship or friendship, we must realize that our words are capable of causing separation, wounding others and even severing relationships.

All of these reasons should impress on us the great responsibility we have as Christians to flood our speech with kindness and respect. After all, despite its small size, our tongue is a mighty tool. We have tiny MP3 players that can play and store thousands of songs; computers that can process massive amounts of information; and shiny boxes that cook our food instantly. We have smartphones and smart cars. And yet, in all their glory, there is no instrument as powerful as the tongue, because no other instrument has so much potential to praise or curse, to repair or destroy. You have been entrusted with a tremendous tool, and it is my prayer, and God's heart, that you use it solely for His purposes.

I can't think of anyone who knew that message better than my beloved friend, the legendary basketball coach John Wooden, to whom this book is dedicated. I had the great honor of knowing Coach personally, and I was at his side up until the very moment he went to be with his Lord. Following his death—which was just a few months before his one hundredth birthday—I was privileged to speak at his memorial service at the University of California, Los Angeles, along with basketball greats such as Kareem Abdul Jabbar and Jamal Wilkes, Al Michaels and Vin Scully. The atmosphere at the service was one of rejoicing and celebrating Coach's remarkable life.

I will never forget how moving the memorial service was, as thousands filled UCLA's Pauley Pavilion (still thousands more tuned in nationally via television and Internet broadcast) to show their appreciation for Coach Wooden. It was obvious how much he was loved, how many lives he had touched and how great his testimony was. Few men are laid to rest with such tender and total adoration.

Coach lived his life as a man who truly pursued righteousness with all that was in him, and this was especially evident in his speech. He would never, ever swear. No turnover ever caused a foul word to be spoken under his breath. No coarse language was necessary to drive his athletes toward one of his 10 national championships. No bad call compromised his word choice. Anyone who has ever been around athletics knows what a rarity this is.

Coach knew that every word counted. He knew about the power the tongue possessed. He knew that living a life of righteousness started with the small things, and so he committed himself to uttering every word as if he were speaking to God Himself. He maintained a pure mouth, and as James affirms, a pure life followed.

If we want to live pure and holy lives, the best place to start is with our speech. Therefore, we turn to James 3:1-12, the go-to section for those who are tired of their speech and desire a holier and more edifying alternative. From this text, we can download an app to curb profanity, transforming our speech from poisonous parlance to profitable praise.

## BEGIN DOWNLOAD

0%    10%   20%   30%   40%   50%   60%   70%   80%   90%

## Step 1: Remember, Only You Can Prevent Forest Fires

Southern California is prone to wildfires due to its hot and arid climate. Add high winds to the mix, which are typical in my neck of the woods, and you've got a recipe for disaster. I've seen a few wildfires. One even came to within 50 yards of our property.

If you have never been near a wildfire, it is difficult to understand the experience; but imagine smoke and ash darkening the sky, blocking the sun from sight and turning the world into grim hues of orange and brown. Ash floats down like snowflakes, covering cars and trees, and even seeps through tiny cracks in windows and doors to enter your home. This, coupled with the amount of smoke in the atmosphere, makes breathing very difficult. You'll see many people donning facemasks, attempting to filter out the smoky air as much as possible. Hundreds and even thousands of residents can be forced to leave their homes when a wildfire threatens, often with little time to gather any precious belongings, and unsure if their homes will be spared.

Just a few years ago, during a devastating forest fire, our church served as a rescue shelter where families could take refuge. At night, it seemed as if the entire landscape was engulfed in flames creeping down the mountains of our San Fernando Valley toward the basin filled with residents. I'll never forget looking out my bedroom window and seeing the ravaging blaze just across the street, praying that the flying embers wouldn't reach our rooftop.

Truly, it is a humbling experience to have no control over such a big and powerful force. And yet, what humbles me most is the fact that this terrain-altering, life-terrorizing force of nature ignites from only a single spark. From a tiny flare comes a conflagration capable of swallowing miles and miles of vegetation and wildlife, and destroying everything else in its path. So, it's not a far step for me to understand what James meant when he wrote: "Consider what a great forest is set on fire by a small spark. The tongue also is a fire, a world of evil among the parts of the body. It corrupts the whole body, sets the whole course of one's life on fire, and is itself set on fire by hell" (Jas. 3:5-6).

In verse 3, James also compares the tongue to the bit a person places in the mouth of a horse to steer the animal; and in verse 4, he compares the tongue to the rudder of a ship. James uses these images to demonstrate that even something as small and seemingly insignificant as the tongue can have a massive impact.

The first step toward downloading this app comes when we recognize the power of our speech. With this in mind, James wrote in verse 2: "We all stumble in many ways. Anyone who is never at fault in what they say is perfect, able to keep their whole body in check." The words we speak carry enough weight to break our backs, if we're not careful. Since this is true, we must do everything in our power to protect our speech. Like watchmen protecting a town's walls from attack, we must be vigilant over our speech, because if the tongue falls, the whole body falls.

In the same way, as we attempt to curb our profanity, we must realize the kind of power with which we're dealing. On November 18, 1956,

Soviet premier Nikita Khrushchev addressed Western ambassadors in Moscow. During a particularly passionate speech, Khrushchev declared that he believed Communism would overtake colonialism, stating, "Whether you like it or not, history is on our side. We will dig you in." He was alluding to digging a grave in which to bury colonialism as deep as possible, but when his Russian was translated to English, the ambassadors heard, "We will bury you!"[2]

These words were spoken during the Cold War, so naturally many took Khrushchev's comment to mean that Russia planned to bury the United States through nuclear bombing.[3] As you can imagine, this statement caused more than a little panic. In fact, it only deepened the chasm between the United States and Russia and served as another bridge they would have to build if they were to cross toward peace.

It's interesting how four words could cause that much panic, and yet this is the power of words. Of course, many of us will never find ourselves in a prominent political office, capable of igniting a war with a single comment, but our words do have the power to bring destruction on a much smaller scale. For instance, a single curse word spoken in the wrong setting could irreparably wreck a person's trustworthiness. One glib comment to a spouse might be the straw that breaks the camel's back and leads to a bitter divorce. A piece of "innocent" gossip could destroy someone's carefully established reputation.

Like it or not, we stand and fall by our words. Though they may seem trivial, they carry the potential to set an entire life on fire and reduce it to ashes. Therefore, we must recognize the scope of the task before us. If we're not careful, we can set spiritual forest fires that cause untold destruction.

**DOWNLOAD IN PROGRESS**

0%   10%   20%   30%   40%   50%   60%   70%   80%   90%

## Step 2: Deflate the Puffer Fish

Among the fish of the sea, there are none quite as interesting as the puffer fish. Normally, the puffer is a very small fish that can evade most predators by using its impressive speed to skirt the hunter's attack. However, when the puffer cannot run away, it fills its stretchy stomach with water and inflates itself to a much larger size. If this doesn't deter the predator, then its poison-filled spines certainly will! In fact, the puffer's poison is believed to be the second deadliest in the world, easily capable of killing a human.[4]

I find the puffer fish to be a unique metaphor for the tongue. While it is inflated, its purpose is to attack others or to appear menacing; and when it attacks, it can inject poison. James wrote that though the tongue is small, it makes great boasts (see Jas. 3:5). The Greek word for "making great boasts" means to brag excessively or exaggerate to inflate the ego. Essentially, the tongue is a muscle flexed by pride.

James seems to assert that pride is the root of the problem with damaging speech. How much of what we say is intended to paint ourselves in a better light? David wondered aloud about people who have the tendency to puff themselves up with their words: "Why do you boast of evil, you mighty hero? Why do you boast all day long, you who are a disgrace in the eyes of God? You who practice deceit, your tongue plots destruction; it is like a sharpened razor" (Ps. 52:1-2).

I've experienced this kind of razor-like language firsthand in sporting events across the country—profane, in-your-face words aimed at inciting anger and discord. Take, for example, a college basketball game this last year at Pauley Pavilion during the regular season between the rivals USC and UCLA. The thrill of the game was cheapened because the students of UCLA began to chant: "F*** USC! F*** USC!" I was appalled when I heard about this the next day via the newspapers and talk radio, and I wondered if the school administrators were equally taken aback. But since this kind of language is so common today, I'm not sure that anyone was offended in the slightest.

The irony is that the same night, I had been at another basketball game between two Christian schools: Azusa Pacific University and Biola University. As I watched the Azusa Pacific team make quick work of Biola, the Azusa fans began to chant: "This is our house! This is our house!" But then, those in the Biola stands chanted back: "This is God's house! This is God's house!"

I was so encouraged by the students of Biola because they understood the key to deflating the tongue's pompous boasts! They understood that God was number one in their gym regardless of who was playing, and that giving Him glory in that moment was more important than winning the game. They understood that the battle against this prideful foe—the tongue—begins when we place ourselves in a position of humility.

I always laugh when I think about a friend of mine from high school who swore all the time. I finally told him that if we were going to continue to hang out, he was going to have to stop cussing. So he and I made a deal that was perfectly suited for a couple of high school boys: Every time he cussed, I got to hit him. It didn't take him long to utter his first curse word after our little deal, so I fulfilled my duty as his accountability partner and punched him in the arm. As soon as I hit him, he yelled out another curse word, so I hit him again. He cursed, so I hit him again, followed by another curse word, followed by another hit. He finally yelled out, "Why are you hitting me?!" I reminded him of our agreement, and miraculously, from that day forward, I never heard my friend use foul language again.

Now, I am not suggesting that you follow our strategy, which is reflective of a 17-year-old's brilliance; but I am suggesting that you determine exactly what you need to do in order to become a person of pure speech. For starters, take some time to make a list of improper things you've recently said to others, and then use this week to make up for those harmful comments by replacing them with encouragement. Ask your neighbors to repeat back to you any hurtful statements or bad jokes you've told. Record yourself over a day's time and play back the recording to find out when you're speaking well and when you're allowing your tongue to flex its pride. Get a jar and place a dollar inside it every time you use a swear word, then donate the money to the charity of your choice.

Whatever the method, recognize that pride is the source of the tongue's power over our lives. Therefore, the more we seek to humble ourselves before others, the more quickly that puffer fish will deflate, allowing us to live peacefully with one another. This is the second, most important step to curb profanity.

**DOWNLOAD IN PROGRESS**

0%   10%   20%   30%   40%   50%   60%   70%   80%   90%

## Step 3: Count the Calories

There is a phrase in the field of computer science called "Garbage in, garbage out," or "GIGO." Coined by George Fuechsel, an IBM technician and instructor in New York, GIGO is used primarily to describe how computers will unquestioningly process the most nonsensical of input data (garbage in) and produce nonsensical output (garbage out). It was most popular in the early days of computing, but it applies even today, when powerful computers are capable of spewing out loads of erroneous information in a short time.[5]

Though we are infinitely more complex than a computer, we are subject to this same principle—especially in our spiritual lives. Whatever enters our eyes and ears, whether it's goodness or garbage, will ultimately flow into our hearts and come out of our mouths. In the Gospel of Luke, Jesus draws our attention to this very topic: "A good man brings good things out of the good stored up in his heart, and an evil man brings evil things out of the evil stored up in his heart. For out of the mouth speaks what the heart is full of" (Luke 6:45).

That being the case, we ought to constantly fuel ourselves with good things and guard what we allow ourselves to see and hear. In Philippians 4:8, the apostle Paul wrote: "Finally, brothers and sisters, whatever is true, whatever is noble, whatever is right, whatever is pure, whatever is lovely, whatever is admirable—if anything is excellent or praiseworthy—think about such things."

Consider the variety of language you expose yourself to every day through movies, magazines, conversations with friends, lyrics to music on your iPod. Imagine using the passage in Philippians 4:8 as a checklist against the media you listen to and watch. Which boxes would you check?

Are your favorite movies, television shows, acquaintances and music . . .

- [ ] True?
- [ ] Noble?
- [ ] Right?
- [ ] Pure?
- [ ] Lovely?
- [ ] Excellent?
- [ ] Admirable?
- [ ] Lovely?

If so, congratulations! These are exactly the sort of things that God wants you to take in with your eyes, ears, mind and heart as a believer. And these things will naturally flow into your heart and out of your mouth.

First Corinthians 15:33 says, "Do not be misled: 'Bad company corrupts good character.'" When we spend our time engaged with movies saturated in violence, music filled with expletives and television shows chock-full of gossip and degrading humor, we are placing ourselves in extremely bad company. It's much like hanging out with a group of bad influences. Over time, their character will imprint onto yours. So if you are exposing your eyes and ears to spiritual garbage, you must be ruthless about taking the garbage out to the curb.

The undeniable principle of "Garbage in, garbage out" is very similar to the saying "You are what you eat." Therefore, our third step in curbing profanity should be to count the calories. Take an honest inventory of the kinds of material you are feeding your eyes and ears. Feed yourself with good, nourishing material that can enrich your soul, and cut out the fatty, unhealthy materials that will only stunt your spiritual growth.

Clean words flow from a clean heart. If you speak foul, perverse words, you must also assume that foul, perverse things also exist in your heart. As a believer in the Lord Jesus Christ, this should not be the case.

## Step 4: Stick a Cork in It

While we must strive for purity in our speech, it's important to note that none of us will be able to completely control our language. Just as we will always fall short of perfection in the way we live, we will also continually falter in our speech. James 3 refers to the tongue as "a world of evil among the parts of the body" in verse 6 and as "a restless evil" in verse 8. That doesn't sound too comforting, does it? Then, in Proverbs 6:16-20, there is a list of seven sins that the Lord absolutely *hates*, and at least three of them directly involve speech.

So if the tongue is so sinful, how can we possibly stop it? How can we bridle what James calls a restless evil? One answer may be found in silence. Many of the early Christians would practice silent meditation and prayer in an effort to control their speech. If we wish to curb our profanity, at times we just need to stick a cork in it. Be quiet. Stop talking.

Let's try a little exercise. Put down this book and be silent for the next five minutes. Try not to think and try not to speak. Just be quiet for a while.

It's hard, isn't it? Author Richard Foster goes even further by challenging his readers in his book *Celebration of Discipline* to undergo an entire day without speaking. He writes, "Note your feelings of helplessness and excessive dependence upon words to communicate. Try to find new ways to relate to others that are not dependent upon words. Enjoy, savor the day. Learn from it."[6] After spending an entire day in silence (if you can do it!), you'll quickly learn how much we depend upon the tongue in everyday life. To go one day without using it can be agony. But we must set out to control our speech instead of allowing it to control us.

In my opinion, we could all stand to be a little more introverted. It's strange, but this world values people who are talkative and quick-witted. Yet, these are rarely the people who find themselves in positions of successful leadership. Business consultant and author Jim Collins, in his book *Good to Great*, which tracks 11 companies that made the leap from average success to outstanding success, noticed something very important about the leadership at each company. These were not rock-star celebrity CEOs who used personal charisma and dynamic speaking skills to command the companies. By and large, these companies were led by people who were quiet and maintained humility.

Colman M. Mockler Jr., the former CEO of Gillette, was a quiet and reserved man, and very much the gentleman. Yet this was the man who led his company to greatness, inventing the Mach-3 and Sensor razors, both of which are still popular among men today. Collins also found similar qualities among the leading executives in his study.[7]

Many people today consider silence a weakness. They believe it means you have nothing to say. But this certainly isn't true. Earlier in the book of James, our author implored us to "be quick to listen, slow to speak" (1:19). To be honest, I think we could all stand to listen more and speak less, even in everyday conversation. If we gave more thought to what we say, I'm certain that we would be better equipped to rein in the "restless evil" that James describes.

In Psalm 17:3, King David made this earnest claim: "Though you probe my heart, though you examine me at night and test me, you will find that I have planned no evil; my mouth has not transgressed." Sometimes that resolution may mean that you keep quiet. If you need to curb your profanity, it's imperative that you stick a cork in it.

**DOWNLOAD IN PROGRESS**

0%   10%   20%   30%   40%   50%   60%   70%   80%   90%

## Step 5: Crack the Whip

Silence cannot completely contain the tongue. James is quick to point this out when he writes, "All kinds of animals, birds, reptiles and sea creatures are being tamed and have been tamed by mankind, but no human being can tame the tongue" (Jas. 3:7-8). The Greek word for "tame" means "to reduce to stillness or quietness,"[8] like when a lion tamer brings the beast's roaring to a stop.

A few years back, in Ventura, California, a county that neighbors Los Angeles, there was quite a commotion over a large cat that had escaped from private captivity. For three weeks, locals reported ominous paw prints on their property and on walking trails. Though unsure of the species, experts had estimated that the wild cat weighed between 400 and 600 pounds, based on the size of the tracks, and had been roaming over an area of 16 square miles.

The excitement reached a peak when one of my daughter's classmates woke up one morning to find an enormous Siberian tiger in her backyard. Authorities were immediately notified and, sadly, to prevent the animal from fleeing toward the nearby park or freeway and harming humans, the tiger was put down.

Shortly thereafter, Gert and Roena Hedengran were arrested for having lied to investigators about their involvement with the tiger. This couple, at one point, privately housed 22 exotic cats. I am more of a dog lover myself, but even for the greatest of cat lovers, owning a tiger or any other large cat seems absolutely crazy. An animal of such size and power does not belong anywhere but in the wild. By nature, this animal simply is not meant to be tamed. And yet, James essentially warns us that we would be better off trying to tame a wild tiger than trying to tame the tongue.

Whenever we speak, we would do well to remember Ephesians 4:29, which says: "Do not let any unwholesome talk come out of your mouths, but only what is helpful for building others up according to their needs, that it may benefit those who listen." The original Greek translation of this verse gives us insight into Paul's wordplay. The word "unwholesome" can also mean "destructive," and the word "helpful" could also mean "constructive." Therefore, a better translation would be: Do not let *destructive* talk come out of your mouths, but only what is *constructive* according to their needs, that it may benefit those who listen. Or, in even simpler terms, don't speak to tear someone down. Speak to build someone up. Say what is in their best interest.

Geoffrey Canada, an education specialist, has been working in the Harlem, New York, school district for years, and he is convinced of the power of positive, constructive speech. During an interview featured on the podcast *This American Life*, he explained the problems that Harlem has suffered from gang violence and poverty, by citing research from childhood development studies. According to these studies, the difference between parents who raised successful children and those who raised problem children wasn't their social class or their race or their neighborhood. The difference was actually in how many positive words the children heard while growing up. Successful children typically heard about 500,000 encouraging words and only 80,000 discouraging words. On the other hand, problem children grew up hearing only an average of 80,000 encouraging words and over 200,000 discouraging words.[9]

How incredible is that? And it's so simple! If we want others to be successful, we must encourage our friends and neighbors with our words.

From time to time, I meet people who come across as extremely negative; who are constantly tearing someone down. Out of love, I have never hesitated to bring that person into my office for the purpose of confronting him or her about it, and I will say, "I have noticed that just about every word that comes out of your mouth is negative." Usually, the person is shocked when I say that, but it surprises the person even more when he or she realizes that someone perceives him/her in this light. I challenge the person to be the man or woman who is always positive, to become the most optimistic person in town. Amazingly, I have seen it work more often than not. I've actually witnessed pessimism in these people turn to optimism. All it took was an honest discussion and a stirring challenge.

The tongue, in the end, can neither be tamed nor silenced. But like a lion tamer who attempts to quiet a ferocious lion, we must do our utmost to rein in our speech. In this way, we will leave our destructive talk behind, replacing it with constructive and beneficial words that build others up.

## Step 6: Get a Bigger Boat

In 1975, audiences all over the country cringed and screamed as they viewed Spielberg's classic film *Jaws*. Watching it many years later, I'm still frightened in spite of the outdated special effects. The most terrifying part of the movie is obviously the three-ton shark itself. When the main character, police chief Martin Brody, finally comes face to face with the monster, he is scared speechless. All he can do is back up from the edge of the deck and muster the courage to say to Sam Quint, a local professional shark hunter, "I think you're going to need a bigger boat."

When you and I are dealing with the monster that our mouth can become, we, too, are going to need a bigger boat. As we discussed earlier, James 3:1-12 elucidates that taming the tongue is impossible, that it is a world of evil with the capacity to wreak havoc. In a spiritual sense, we might imagine the tongue as some monster shark rampaging the waters and leaving destroyed lives in its wake.

In James 3:10-12 of our text, James uses the imagery of water to illustrate the dichotomy of the tongue. After pointing out the hypocrisy of using one's mouth to both praise God and curse men, he writes, "Out of the same mouth come praise and cursing. My brothers and sisters, this should not be. Can both fresh water and salt water flow from the same spring? My brothers and sisters, can a fig tree bear olives, or a grapevine bear figs? Neither can a salt spring produce fresh water." What does this mean exactly? It means that goodness and wickedness cannot come from the same source.

When we think about *Jaws*, we picture a massive and terrifying shark, which is also an appropriate symbol for the salt water it inhabits: cold, heartless and all consuming. Moreover, it symbolizes what I think it means to have "saltwater lives," speaking words that in the end are cold, heartless and all consuming.

We learned in chapter 3, when we downloaded God's app to break down the walls that divide, that faith and favoritism do not mix. Likewise, there is a great contradiction when both good and bad words flow from the mouths of those who profess to be Christians. Thus, it should be impossible for curse words or critical speech to come from the mouth of a believer.

How many times have you left the church parking lot—after singing worship songs, shouting "Amen!" at the good parts of the sermon and saying "God bless you" as you pass fellow congregants in the hallways—only to cuss out the first person who cuts you off on the road? Some of us don't even wait to *leave* the church parking lot before our cursing begins, and it continues throughout the week at work, home or school.

My friend, this should not be. Christ does not call us to this kind of life. He desires that our speech be fresh and pristine—characterized by words filled with wisdom from the Scriptures and grace that nourishes others like a stream of life-sustaining and thirst-quenching water. So, then, how do we uncover a spring of cold and fresh water in our speech? By filling our mouths with prayer and praise. I've always believed that God inhabits the praise of His people and that He shows up precisely when we speak His glorious name aloud or voice our admiration of Him. If we allow this fresh water to flow from our speech, then we will soon see the harsh, salty water dissipate from our lives.

This is the way you place yourself in a "bigger boat" and become able to defeat the beast lurking in the salty depths. Don't you want to be the kind of person who is recognized in your community and workplace as someone who consistently gives the glory back to God in your speech? By devoting yourself to praising the Lord, you will cut loose the monster shark threatening to cause destruction in others' lives and sail down the peaceful waters of God's amazing compassion and grace. As you download this final step of this app, release the saltwater monster into the wild and become a person who is characterized by the fresh, eternal fountain of God's love.

In this chapter, you've discovered these six steps toward downloading God's app for curbing profanity:

- Prevent forest fires by understanding the power the tongue holds over the rest of the body. Just as a small spark can ignite a flame and reduce a forest to ashes, the tongue has the potential to destroy entire lives.
- Discover the source of the tongue's power, which is pride. By defusing our arrogance, we deflate the boasts of our tongue to manageable proportions.

- Keep track of your spiritual intake. The more profanity and coarse joking and gossip you listen to or watch, the more likely you'll be to take part in this unpardonable language.
- Get silent before God. One method for containing your speech is to refuse to speak at all, choosing first to listen either to the Father or to others. In this way, you are able to respond with wisdom and understanding.
- Crack the whip by rejecting harmful speech and choosing to speak constructively toward others. While it is impossible to completely silence the tongue, you can guide it so that your words will build others up rather than tear them down.
- Step into a bigger boat while saturating your speech in prayer and praise. In this way, you will flood out the cursing and coarse joking from your vocabulary and replace it with pure, acceptable speech before your Father.

As you apply these practical steps and suggestions to your everyday life, my prayer is that you will notice a marked change in the way you interact with people around you. Undoubtedly, they will notice it as well, because you will bless them with words that are seasoned with love and encouragement. You will gain a reputation as a person who is positive and edifying, and the Lord God Almighty will be glorified through your speech. Amen!

# God Has an App to
# Restore a Broken Heart

## James 4:1-12

Rudolf and Adolf Dassler created an empire in their mother's laundry room in the 1920s. Growing up in the small Bavarian town of Herzogenaurach, the two brothers started a shoe company—using pedal power from a stationary bicycle to run their equipment whenever electricity was unreliable. Rudolf was the assertive salesman while Adolf thoughtfully crafted the lightweight athletic shoes; the two seemed to be the perfect team.[1]

Soon, the Dassler Brothers Shoe Factory moved out of "Mom's house" and into a more suitable location. Their designs leaped onto the world stage at the 1936 Summer Olympics in Berlin when they provided footwear for U.S. sprinter Jesse Owens, who won four gold medals. Having cemented their reputation and relationships with some of the most famous sportsmen and trainers worldwide, business suddenly boomed for Rudolf and Adolf.[2]

Sometime after World War II, things went sour between the brothers. Many speculate that Rudolf wasn't happy that Adolf may have gone behind his back to secure the sponsorship with Jesse Owens. Others theorize that the rift had to do with political differences and an affiliation with the Nazi party, while others think it could have had something to do with their wives or a simple misunderstanding in a bomb shelter. To this day, no one knows for sure what caused the brothers' fallout, but in 1948, the Dassler Brothers Shoe Factory was split in two—and so was the town of Herzogenaurach.

It's rumored that Rudolf packed his bags in the middle of the night and moved his family to the other side of the Aurach River. He started his own shoe company called "Puma," while Adolf patented the name "Adidas," which is a combination of his nickname "Adi" and the first three letters of his last name. The feud between the Dasslers lasted for decades, tearing their family apart and deeply dividing their hometown—with the quiet Aurach River symbolizing a wall of separation between Rudolf's supporters on one bank and Adolf's on the other. Today, this little town in northern Bavaria is nicknamed the "place of bent necks" because everyone checks out everyone else's shoes before they will start a conversation.[3] Talk about brand loyalty!

Sadly, the brothers who founded two of the largest athletic shoe and apparel companies in the world never reconciled. Though they are buried in the same cemetery, their graves are as far apart as possible.[4] The Dassler brothers died harboring resentment and an irreparably broken relationship with one another.

What is more tragic is that this story has been repeated over and over again, across the ages and around the world—wives and husbands divorce, parents become estranged from their children, brother contends with brother, sisters stop speaking to one another, and longtime friendships dissolve bitterly. Each person is left resentful and brokenhearted and, like the Dassler brothers, may not even remember what caused the fight in the first place.

If you were able to see inside every person you passed by on the highways, byways and walkways of your city, I have no doubt that you would notice a conspicuous fracture upon just about every heart. What's the main cause? Shattered relationship bonds between people who once loved one another.

Some relationships seem to be unable to stand the test of time or overcome conflict. Yet, God has created every man and woman with the desire to form lasting, loving and meaningful relationships. Reflect on the relationships in your own life for a moment. If you are married, your spouse is likely your chief priority. If you are single, your friends take on an enormous role in your life. You surely cherish your parents, grandparents, children, siblings and even your pets. You bond with teammates and classmates, and you build relationships in the workplace.

You and I are relational beings created in the image of a relational God, and this intrinsic quality of God's nature is immediately revealed to us in the very beginning of Scripture. Genesis 1:26 tells us, "Then God said, 'Let us make mankind in our image, in our likeness.' " Though it's easy to miss, notice the important reference to God's triune being in the words "us" and "our." Notice that He does not say "Let me make man in my image, in my likeness." Instead, the words "us" and "our" indicate the very existence of God as a special union between the Father, Son and Holy Spirit—also known as the Trinity.

Revealing the three manifestations of the same God in perfect relationship with each other, the Trinity shows us that God, within His own identity, is relational. I know this concept may be a deep and difficult one to grasp, but it's extremely relevant. You see, God by nature is wholly and entirely relational and loving toward His children because He is wholly and entirely relational and loving within His own being.

And get this: From the Genesis text just mentioned, we also glean that God chose to create us so that He might fulfill His relational nature *through a relationship with us*. Having been made in His image, we, too, are relational and, therefore, capable of being in relationship with Him and with others. Because the catalyst of our creation came from God's relational makeup, it is easy to see why relationships are at our very core.

Since relationships lie at the center of humanity, they seem to possess an unequivocal power to make or break us. They move, drive and inspire us. They can elicit overwhelming joy or unbearable devastation. In fact, the sad reality is that, though we were made to be in healthy and harmonious relationship with one another, the opposite is often true. Instead of establishing uplifting, long-lasting, God-honoring bonds, our lives are sometimes bogged down by discouraging, unstable, unhealthy unions.

Every year, I receive countless letters from people whose hearts are immensely burdened. More often than not, the cause is relational discord—they are experiencing marital trouble or their children aren't getting along or there is dissent between them and another family member, co-worker or friend. So, if broken relationships are the cause of broken hearts, what then is the root of broken relationships? Through James 4:1-12, God identifies four sources of the strife that demolishes the harmony between people.

## The Desires that Battle Within Us

James first asks, "What causes fights and quarrels among you? Don't they come from your desires that battle within you?" (Jas. 4:1). Right off the bat, our author incontrovertibly points out that the tension in our relationships comes from selfishly desiring what we don't have. This is called covetousness, as James explains in verse 2: "You desire but do not have, so you kill. You covet but you cannot get what you want, so you quarrel and fight."

Think about it: Most of our arguments result from not getting what we want. I know two families who live next door to each other but they despise one another because one neighbor built a fence that the other neighbor thought was ugly. One household wanted the fence, the other one didn't. Neither would budge. How pitiful that a measly fence would cause a 10-year feud between two families!

In more extreme cases, James says that some people will even kill when they don't get their way. Of the 13,636 murders in the U.S. in 2009, for which the circumstance surrounding the murder was known, 41.2 percent of victims were murdered during arguments (including romantic triangles). Felony circumstances (i.e., robbery and burglary) accounted for 22.9 percent of murders.[5] Tragically, the darkest capability of mankind is exposed as a result of an intense desire for something we can't have.

The struggle to get what we want isn't limited to physical objects. Recall the reason for the last argument you were part of. Did you feel that someone had overstepped your boundaries, ripped you off or neglected you? Did you feel that you were not being respected? We all have expectations that are not met, and this is the origin of so many of our arguments.

When I was growing up, my mom did all of our yard work. She mowed the lawn, pulled the weeds, watered the flowers—she did it all. My wife, on the other hand, grew up in a home where her brother was responsible for mowing their yard. We never discussed this before we got married, and we each expected that the other would be in charge of the yard. It was actually a surprise when we became aware of each other's unmet expectations on this issue. For this very reason, we have a gardener!

In all seriousness, focusing on unmet expectations—such as yard work, finances, extended family—can lead to destroyed relationships. We all have wants that go unfulfilled, and for this reason, the first step in downloading the app to restore a broken heart is to take a good long look at the selfish desires that battle within us and work on reducing their importance.

## Our Failure to Ask God

Second, James asserts, "You do not have because you do not ask God" (4:2). This reminds me of an important point Jesus made during His preeminent Sermon on the Mount, recorded in Mathew 5-7. As He made His way through Galilee, Christ taught in the synagogues, proclaimed the gospel and healed every kind of illness among the people. As His reputation spread to Syria, a country bordering Israel to the northeast, those who were sick, suffering, paralyzed and demon-possessed were brought to Him for healing. The Bible says that large crowds from across the land followed Him (see Matt. 4:23-25), so Jesus went up and sat on a mountainside and began to teach them. Take a look at what He said, according to Matthew 7:7-8:

> Ask and it will be given to you; seek and you will find; knock and the door will be opened to you. For everyone who asks receives; the one who seeks finds; and to the one who knocks, the door will be opened.

Immediately following these words, Christ posed a couple of hypothetical questions:

Which of you, if your son asks for bread, will give him a stone? Or if he asks for a fish, will give him a snake? If you, then, though you are evil, know how to give good gifts to your children, how much more will your Father in heaven give good gifts to those who ask him! (vv. 9-11).

Like a good father, God desires to give us what we need! But when we have a broken heart or relationship that needs restoration, how many of us are driven to our knees to ask the Lord for help? Isn't it astonishing to think that we've made a mess of certain relational conflicts because we've tried to solve them on our own? We act and react out of pride and selfishness, and fail to ask the One who can give us a holy and humble perspective. Perhaps our relationships are broken because we've failed to ask God to fix them.

## A Selfish Shopping List

Third, a sobering reality is pointed out in James 4:3: "When you ask, you do not receive, because you ask with wrong motives, that you may spend what you get on your pleasures." As James highlights, the selfishness that pollutes our relationships can even seep into our prayer life. Turning to God is a huge first step in restoration, but all too often, we haven't yet abandoned our impure motives, and we actually pray selfishly.

When I was preparing for ministry at Ozark Christian College, I spent a lot of time with a good friend of mine named Larry Bryant, who was a gifted songwriter. Larry wrote a tongue-in-cheek song about this very issue, capturing how ridiculous it is when we choose to pray selfishly. Take a look at these lyrics. (To listen, please visit www.GodHasAnApp.com.)

Lord, I need to talk to You
There's so much on my heart
So many burdens make it hard
to know just where to start.

Thank You for Your family
Your mercy and Your love
Now on to more important things
I'll give my magic lamp a rub:

Give me this, I want that
Bless me, Lord, I pray
Grant me what I think I need
to make it through the day.

Make me wealthy,
Keep me healthy,
Fill in what I missed
on my never-ending shopping list.

Lord, You've been so good to me
How could I ask for more?
But since You said to ask, I will
'cause what else is prayer for?

The cattle on a thousand hills
They all belong to You.
I don't need any cows right now
But something else might do.

I want a nice white smile on a perfect face
and perfect hair that will stay in place.
I want a smaller nose and a single chin
and a figure like a perfect ten
And a mom that never yells or screams
and hips that fit in designer jeans

And a tennis court and a heated pool
I could use them, Lord, as a witnessing tool.
And a color TV and a VCR
and Jesus plates on a brand new car.[6]

Though Larry's song is catchy and humorous, it reveals a sad truth about the attitude with which we approach God when it comes to our desires. Our heavenly Father is not a magic genie in a lamp. He is the Almighty God who cares about our problems and our needs, but He will not gratify our sinful requests to our own detriment. Asking God for something from the wrong motive is yet another cause of our broken relationships.

## Friendship with the World

Our final cause of broken relationships involves an unhealthy association with the world. James writes, "You adulterous people, don't you know that friendship with the world means enmity against God? Therefore, anyone who chooses to be a friend of the world becomes an enemy of God" (4:4). It's hard to ignore the severity of these words as James calls our attention to this serious and divisive issue.

James likens friendship with the world to adultery. Just as a man or woman betrays his or her spouse by having a physical affair, we are unfaithful to God when we dabble in earthly exploits. What exactly constitutes friendship with the world? Paul provides an important checklist in 1 Corinthians 6:9-11, explaining that sexual immorality, idolatry (which is putting anything or anyone above the Lord in our estimation and affections), stealing, greed, drunkenness, slander and cheating are all things that God's people have been cleansed of through salvation in Christ Jesus. To return to such worldly vices is to befriend the world again and to be disloyal to God.

Next, James equates "friendship with the world" with "hatred toward God." This may seem like quite a heavy comparison, but it is echoed in 1 John 2:15-16. Read the following words carefully—two or three times if you must:

> Do not love the world or anything in the world. If anyone loves the world, love for the Father is not in them. For everything in the world—the lust of the flesh, the lust of the eyes, and the pride of life—comes not from the Father but from the world.

You and I belong to God. We have been bought by the blood of His Son, Jesus Christ. Attempting to maintain a friendship with the world goes against the very Spirit of Him who dwells within us. When both of these forces are in direct conflict with one another, it is the final source of disharmony in our relationship with God and with others.

Broken relationships seem to permeate every church, household, schoolyard and workplace. God is not blind to humanity's epidemic of shattered hearts, and He cares deeply about heart restoration. In fact, when we fail to live in proper relationship with Him and with each other, we are actually missing out on a huge part of His design for our lives.

For this very reason, God has included in His Word an app to restore the broken heart. As we continue dissecting James 4, we are presented with a life-changing opportunity to kneel down and pick up the fragments of our brokenness, so that the Lord can slowly but surely piece us back together and prepare us for relationships that truly please Him. In this text, we discover six steps to download God's app for restoration.

**BEGIN DOWNLOAD**

0%    10%    20%    30%    40%    50%    60%    70%    80%    90%

## Step 1: Unfriend an Old Friend

Has there ever been a time when it was easier to make friends? With the advent of Facebook, you could spend hour after hour searching for current acquaintances, old friends from high school and college and a bunch of other people you may or may not know; and before the day was through you could end up with hundreds of "friends." It's kind of exciting, at first, seeing what everyone's been up to and reading the inspiring quotes or funny anecdotes posted.

But after a while, doesn't the thrill wear off a little? You begin to wonder if you're wasting too much time as you question the quality of these "friendships." I mean, is the person truly a friend when you never spend time with him or her but occasionally hit "like" on a clever saying he or she uploaded to the News Feed? Do you care what Ted from elementary school ordered at McDonald's today? Are you frustrated, too, by the person who always seems to share a play-by-play of the game before you've had a chance to watch it? And if you read another post from Julie in Montana about what new vegetable puree her baby consumed, you might just delete your entire account!

Thankfully, you don't have to go to such extreme measures, because the genius engineers at Facebook created a little button that used to be called "Unfriend." Now I think it's simply called "Delete." This special feature allows you to remove from your account any person with whom you no longer want to be in contact. With the click of a button—poof—he or she is gone!

As we revisit James 4:4, we have to apply this same principle to our spiritual lives as a first step to restoring a broken heart. We must "unfriend" the world. To be a friend is to attach yourself to someone "by feelings of affection or personal regard";[7] we are a friend to the world when we show regard for the things of the world that cause men to covet, fight, quarrel, steal and kill.

If Jesus Christ is your Lord and Savior, Ephesians 4:22-24 instructs you to walk away from your former way of life . . . to be made new in the attitude of your minds, and to put on the new self, created to be like God in true righteousness and holiness. When you fail to reject the worldly habits and affinities you used to cherish before you met Jesus, you make yourself an enemy of God and cause the Holy Spirit that dwells within you to yearn jealously for you (see Jas. 4:4-5). You cannot be a true friend of God, or experience restoration with others, unless you unfriend the world.

But, as the old saying goes, breaking up is hard to do. To unfriend the world requires constant vigilance, prayer and meditation on God's Word—filling yourself *daily* with the things of God. It means avoiding certain places or websites you used to visit, songs you used to listen to, movies or television shows you used to watch, books you used to read, friends that are bad influences.

Your success in unfriending the world is made possible through humility and by the grace of God, which James 4:6 makes clear: "But he gives us more grace. That is why Scripture says: 'God opposes the proud but shows favor to the humble.'" Unfriend the world with all diligence and humility. This is the first step in God's app to restore a broken heart.

**DOWNLOAD IN PROGRESS**

0%    10%    20%    30%    40%    50%    60%    70%    80%    90%

## Step 2: Surrender to the Proper Authority

Imagine that you are standing in line at the bank, minding your own business and waiting to make a transaction. Suddenly, you notice a tense commotion ahead of you at the teller window. A man with a gun turns from the counter and heads for the exit with a sack full of cash, but he soon trips on a brass stanchion. The bag of money flings from his grip and lands in *your* hands. Your body is frozen but your heart is racing. *Is this really happening right now?*

Just then, a police officer bursts into the building with his gun drawn. The crook recovers from his fall and stands to his feet, pointing his gun at the cop. You are literally about to get caught in the crossfire. The criminal turns to you and yells, "Toss me the money, or I'll shoot!" But the officer assures you that everything is going to be fine and instructs you to get down on the ground, slowly and easily. Caught between a rock and a hard place, you can't possibly yield to both men. You, my friend, have an important decision to make.

When James 4:7 says, "Submit yourselves, then, to God. Resist the devil, and he will flee from you," it is much like the bank robbery scenario. The officer of the law represents God, and the bank robber represents the devil. You can only trust and surrender to the authority of one or the other—for it's impossible to serve two masters (see Luke 16:13)—and the one you choose will determine how successful you will be in downloading God's app to restore your broken heart.

To submit to God is to yield to His authority in your life. You surrender your will, desires and opinions to His will, His power and His wisdom. If you were suffering from actual heart disease and had the opportunity to be examined by the world's leading cardiologist, would you reject his or her expert diagnosis? I doubt it. In fact, if your life was on the line, my guess is that you would do whatever that doctor told you to do so you could live, whether it was a change in your diet or medication, or a critical surgery. Submitting to God is just like that! You have to obey whatever He tells you to do in His Word, the Bible.

When you submit to God's authority, it's only natural that you will resist the devil and withstand his schemes. But it's also a very deliberate action. Titus 2:12 reveals that God's grace and salvation "teaches us to say 'No' to ungodliness and worldly passions, and to live self-controlled, upright and godly lives in this present age." Therefore, you can effectively resist the enemy simply by saying no—as many times as you must—just like Joseph did (see Gen. 39:7-12) when he tenaciously rejected the advances of his boss's wife. Just as Joseph withstood this treacherous woman, so too you must resist Satan.

When you hold your ground before the enemy, choosing to submit to the proper Authority—the Lord Jesus Christ—James 4:7 promises that the devil will flee from you. Like a wily old bank robber trying to make his escape, your enemy will realize that there's no use trying to steal the joy in your heart. Instead, he will take his loot of pride, covetousness and strife with him, all of which are causes of broken relationships, and leave you one step closer to total restoration.

**DOWNLOAD IN PROGRESS**

0%    10%    20%    30%    40%    50%    60%    70%    80%    90%

## Step 3: Run, Forrest, Run!

It's probably one of the most inspiring scenes in cinematic history. Young Forrest Gump and his friend Jenny are walking home from school along a dirt road when suddenly three boys appear behind them on bicycles. One of them throws a rock that hits Forrest on his head; another one smacks him in the eye, causing him to fall flat on his back. Jenny helps Forrest to his feet and urges him to run away, so Forrest hops to it—as best he can with metal braces on his legs.

"Run, Forrest, run!" Jenny yells, when the three bullies grab their bikes and speed after him.

The frame slows down and zooms in on Forrest's legs, which sway stiffly back and forth, restricted by the braces. The boys on bicycles are gaining on him. Then the orchestra music swells, and we hear the popping sound of the braces loosening and then coming apart. Forrest is soon completely free of his metal bindings and picks up tremendous speed, his legs as graceful as an Olympic champion. He's too fast for the bullies, and they give up their pursuit, while Forrest runs to the safety of his momma's big white house.

Like Forrest Gump, you and I must run to the safety of our heavenly Father when we are suffering from brokenness. He is a shelter for those who put their trust in Him, as King David extols in Psalm 36:7: "How priceless is your unfailing love, O God! People take refuge in the shadow of your wings." Running to the Lord with our broken heart is the third step in our app for restoration, and it is elucidated in James 4:8: "Come near to God and he will come near to you." But how exactly do we come near to God?

We learn from Psalm 145:18 that "the LORD is near to all who call on him, to all who call on him in truth." There are two ways in which you can sincerely call on the Lord: The first is through prayer, daily asking God to restore your broken heart and work out your circumstances; the second is by seeking out His wisdom, carving time out of your schedule to read the Bible. Both of these avenues are readily available to you day or night. God is—and always has been—there for you with open arms, waiting patiently for you to run to Him.

This reminds me of a story about a couple who had been married for a long time and were driving in the car together. Their vehicle was an older model with bench seats, which allowed lovebirds to cuddle close as they cruised the streets. (Nowadays, cars usually have bucket seats in the front that are separated by a center console.) Sitting on opposite sides of the bench seat and reflecting on their years together, the woman said to her husband, "Remember when we were young, how close we used to sit in the car? Now we always sit totally opposite of each other." Her husband turned to her and said, "Well, honey, I've never moved."

So often we wonder why God seems to be so distant when we are hurting; the truth is that He has never moved. If only we would slide over and cuddle next to Him, surely we would find that He's the antidote to our heartbreak. Dear friend, if you are battling brokenness, come near to the One who can dry your tears and restore your heart.

**DOWNLOAD IN PROGRESS**

0%   10%   20%   30%   40%   50%   60%   70%   80%   90%

## Step 4: Find the Fairest of Them All

The queen's beauty was surpassed only by her vanity. Possessing a magical mirror that answered any question honestly, she would gaze at her reflection and ask, "Mirror, mirror on the wall, who in the land is fairest of all?" Each time, the mirror would reply, "You, my queen, are fairest of all." But when the queen's stepdaughter, Snow White, reached maturity, she became exceedingly lovely. On that day, the queen posed her usual inquiry to her mirror, and it responded, "Queen, you are full fair, 'tis true, but Snow White is a thousand times fairer than you."[8]

If only our own mirrors had the ability to speak candidly, like the magic mirror in this Brothers Grimm fairy tale *Snow White and the Seven Dwarves*. Though in reality mirrors can't talk, it would do us a lot of good to look at our reflection whenever we are experiencing brokenness in marriage, friendships and other relationships. If we were to take an honest look in the mirror, we would be able to see and face the truth about our flaws and assume personal responsibility for our failures.

James 4:8 says, "Wash your hands, you sinners, and purify your hearts, you double-minded," which reveals that in order to gain true restoration from the Lord, it is imperative that your hands, heart and mind become free from sin. This is a crucial step in downloading God's app to mend a broken heart, and it involves confessing your offenses to Him.

There are two parts to confession. First and foremost, confession means to acknowledge the truth about God—that He alone is truly righteous, just, holy, graceful, merciful and forgiving. The second part of confession is to tell the truth about ourselves—that we are sinful, prideful, flawed and prone to make mistakes. Our tendency, instead, is to point the finger of blame and accuse others of causing our troubles and our pain. But as the old expression goes, when you point your finger at someone else, you have three fingers pointing back at you. Listen to what Jesus says in Matthew 7:3-5:

> Why do you look at the speck of sawdust in your brother's eye and pay no attention to the plank in your own eye? How can you say to your brother, "Let me take the speck out of your eye," when all the time there is a plank in your own eye? You hypocrite, first take the plank out of your own eye, and then you will see clearly to remove the speck from your brother's eye.

How absurd it would be to allow a surgeon with poor eyesight and dirty hands to operate on you. Likewise, you are not fit to seek restoration until your heart and hands are clean. When you are cleansed by confessing your sins to God, He does something significant in your life, as Psalm 34:18 makes plain: "The LORD is near to those who have a broken heart, and saves such as have a contrite spirit" (*NKJV*). The word "contrite" in this verse means "showing sincere remorse and the desire for atonement."[9] It connotes a humble acknowledgement of sin, which James 4:10 reinforces: "Humble yourselves before the Lord, and he will lift you up."

A brief but important aside: I understand that your broken heart may truly be the result of someone's careless disregard of your feelings and wellbeing, or utter betrayal of your trust and confidence. In situations of abuse, crime and neglect, there is a perpetrator who is 100 percent in the wrong. The key to restoring a broken heart in cases such as these is forgiveness. Dr. Charles Stanley wrote, in a valuable article called "Letting Go of Anger," "Forgive the offender. Unless we release the people who have wronged us, bitterness and resentment will take root in our lives. Only by giving up our right for revenge and restitution can we begin to experience the freedom God desires for His children. As we surrender our hostile feelings to the Lord, His presence will begin to restore and heal our broken hearts."[10]

In cases where two or more parties each share some type of liability, confession is the key. Conflict and divisiveness arise all the time, but you alone control how you respond. When you choose to confess your own transgressions to God, you will be able to see the situation more clearly and accept responsibility for your part. With humility, ask the Lord to show you any sinfulness; and when He does, ask Him to forgive you. When you take an honest look in the mirror and confess your sins, you will find the fairest of them all— your Father in heaven—and you will take a big step toward allowing Him to restore your broken heart.

**DOWNLOAD IN PROGRESS**

0%  10%  20%  30%  40%  50%  60%  70%  80%  90%

## Step 5: Hammer the Clamor

James admonishes us, in 4:11, not to "slander one another" or speak against a brother or sister in any situation. "Slander" is not a word we often hear or use, but it is something we often do. To slander means to intentionally tarnish the name and reputation of someone—basically, to talk bad about a person. When we are brokenhearted and angry, we sometimes respond by slandering the person we feel has hurt us, seeking to repay the damage through our words.

As believers, we are called to choose a better course of action. Ephesians 4:30-32 tells us:

And do not grieve the Holy Spirit of God, by whom you were sealed for the day of redemption. Let all bitterness, wrath, anger, clamor, and evil speaking be put away from you, with all malice. And be kind to one another, tender-hearted, forgiving one another, even as God in Christ forgave you (*NKJV*).

These are great verses to memorize and keep at the core of all your decisions in dealing with conflict and hurt, and there is one particular word I wish to highlight from this passage. The word "clamor" means "a loud uproar" and a "vehement expression of desire or dissatisfaction."[11] Many of us become professional clamorers when we feel that our rights have been violated or when things don't go our way. Do any of these comments sound familiar?

"Mom, that is *so* unfair!"

"Officer, I absolutely was not speeding. I'm going to fight this ticket!"

"That's a terrible call, ref!"

"If he would just admit he was wrong, everything would be fine!"

We are very quick to complain to anyone who will listen, building a case for why we are so right and why the other person is so at fault. Dear friend, this is the very basis of slander, and as we learned from Ephesians 4:30-32, we must put an end to this practice.

Though Jesus suffered the cruelest injustice in all of history—His undeserved death on a Roman cross—He did not protest. As Isaiah 53:7 prophesied, "He was oppressed and afflicted, yet he did not open his mouth; he was led like a lamb to the slaughter, and as a sheep before its shearers is silent, so he did not open his mouth." Jesus Christ was truly innocent of any wrongdoing. And despite being completely and totally sinless, He did not clamor when He was accused, beaten, pierced, insulted, humiliated, spat on and nailed to a cross. He did not plead His case; He simply responded, "Father, forgive them" (Luke 23:34) and laid down His life for you and for me.

Let us follow the amazingly humble and gentle example set forth by our beautiful Savior. When you are in conflict with someone, guard your words carefully so that you do not sin by slandering them. Put an end to arguments and blame by trusting in the One who knows your pain firsthand—the only One who has the ability to heal your hurt and restore your heart.

**DOWNLOAD IN PROGRESS**

■■■■■■■■■■■■■■■■■■■■■■■■■■■■■■■■■■■■■■■■■■■■■■■■■■■

0%     10%    20%    30%    40%    50%    60%    70%    80%    90%

## Step 6: Don't Carry the Donkey

As we come to the final step of our download of God's app to restore a broken heart, we must revisit a familiar concept we tackled in chapter 3 when we broke down the walls that divide: a tendency to judge others. This tendency is a pitfall we must constantly watch out for, and it's the last hindrance to rebuilding relationships and restoring broken hearts. James 4:11 says, "Anyone who speaks against a brother or sister or judges them speaks against the law and judges it. When you judge the law, you are not keeping it, but sitting in judgment on it."

When you choose to judge someone, James is saying that you essentially elevate yourself higher than God and His perfect law. This is immensely foolish and sinful, for as verse 12 continues, "There is only one Lawgiver and Judge, the one who is able to save and destroy. But you—who are you to judge your neighbor?" Rather than striving to live up to the standard of God's Word in your own actions, you require that others live up to your standards and expectations. This imposes ridiculous burdens on others that they cannot bear.

It reminds me of Aesop's fable about an old man and his young son who were walking to town with their donkey. As they strolled beside the donkey, they passed by a few of their countrymen who said, "How foolish you are! What good is that donkey if you're just going to walk? One of you should be riding that donkey." So, the man placed the boy upon the donkey and they continued their journey.

Then they passed another group of men, and one of them said, "Look at that selfish young lad, letting his elderly father walk while he himself rides that donkey!" Hearing this, the boy got off the donkey, his father got on the donkey, and they went on their way. They hadn't gotten far before passing a couple of women who said, "Oh, you are such a lazy man! You're old and strong; you should let the boy ride on the donkey."

The old man and his son looked at each other and decided that they should *both* ride the donkey. As they made their way to town, sure enough someone else came along and said, "You guys are so cruel, so selfish—the both of you on that one little donkey." So, the man and the boy got off the donkey and tried to think of what to do.

They thought and thought until they came up with a plan. The father cut down a sturdy sapling and whittled off the branches so that it became a pole. Then they tied the donkey's feet to the pole and lifted it onto their shoulders, carrying the donkey into town. As you can imagine, the man, the boy and the donkey were met by uproarious laughter as they passed people along the road.

Soon, they came to the Market Bridge, which provided passage across a deep river. But the donkey, getting one of his hooves loose of the ties, kicked out and caused the boy to drop his end of the pole. In the struggle, the donkey fell over the side of the bridge. Since his forefeet were still tied together, the poor animal drowned.[12]

The point of this sad story is that judging others is a slippery slope, leading to unreasonable expectations that cannot be met. When your friends, family, neighbors and co-workers fall short of these expectations, and you exact judgment, it is in contradiction of what Christ calls you to do. Look at His command in Matthew 7:1-2:

> Do not judge, or you too will be judged. For in the same way you judge others, you will be judged, and with the measure you use, it will be measured to you.

This is a serious charge. Quite literally, the way you judge others will determine the way that your Father in heaven judges you. But if you choose mercy and grace—as He did when Christ died on the cross at Calvary for your sins and mine—you will appropriately step down from the judge's seat upon which God alone is worthy and qualified to sit. Trust the Lord to examine the heart and motives of those who have broken your heart, and leave all judgment to Him. You will find that letting go of this responsibility is tremendously liberating, and it will allow God to place the finishing touches of restoration upon your heart.

**DOWNLOAD COMPLETE!**

0%  10%  20%  30%  40%  50%  60%  70%  80%  90%

American writer Barbara Bloom once noted, "When the Japanese mend broken objects, they aggrandize the damage by filling the cracks with gold. They believe that when something's suffered damage and has a history it becomes more beautiful." What a beautiful analogy for what God does with our brokenness!

Having downloaded God's restorative app through careful consideration of the spiritual principles of James 4:1-12, you now see that the Lord is exceedingly and abundantly able to put your broken heart back together to beat once again with beauty, strength and love. As you seek healing in all of your relationships, here are the essentials:

- Unfriend an old friend by relinquishing all affinity for the things of the world through humility and God's grace.
- Surrender to authority, submitting to the Lord and His will for your life.
- Run to God who, in turn, will draw near to you.
- Take an honest look in the mirror and confess your sin to God.
- Hammer the clamor. When you choose not to slander others, you will follow Christ's perfect example.

- Refuse to carry the donkey by putting aside judgment and leaving justice to God.

Dear brokenhearted, please look no further for healing, strength, courage or comfort in all of your relationships. It flows from the veins of Jesus, and it's available to you, just as He designed it from the beginning. Bring all your cares and worries—everything that needs restoration—to Christ, and He will make you whole.

God Has an App to
# Prioritize Your Investments

## James 4:13-17

Leo Tolstoy is often remembered for his epic novel *War and Peace*, but few know that he was a devout Christian and wrote a series of short stories concerning Christian values. In one story called "How Much Land Does a Man Need?" he told about a landowner named Pahom. Now, this landowner was an honest man, not given to gambling or drinking, but he was also a proud man and boasted that he only needed one thing in the world to make him happy: land. He didn't necessarily need much; he just needed enough to provide food and sustenance for himself and his family.

Pahom started out with a good stretch of land, but as year after year passed, he continued to buy up the land of his neighbors until he became content. However, a foreigner came from afar and told Pahom about a distant country where the owners were selling thousands of acres of land at a bargain. It would be easy, the foreigner assured him. All he would have to do is offer gifts to the natives, and they would return the favor by offering to sell him as much land as he wished at a reasonable price. Pahom was intrigued by this story and decided to see if it was true.

It was just as the foreigner said, for Pahom and his servants happened upon a tent-dwelling people in possession of thousands of unused acres. When he offered them gifts, the tent-dwellers were delighted to repay Pahom by selling him some of their land.

He asked the chief how much the land would cost, and the chief replied, "Our price is always the same: one thousand rubles a day."

A thousand rubles a day? That didn't sound quite right. How can you measure land in days? But the chief explained that they had no idea how to measure land except by walking around it. They offered Pahom all the land that he could walk around in one day for a small sum of a thousand rubles. Pahom could hardly contain himself. Without a doubt, this was a steal.

But the chief stated that there was one condition: Pahom could start at sunrise to mark out his land, but if he didn't return to his starting point by sundown, then he would lose all of his money. That was the deal.

Pahom could hardly sleep that night as he thought about all the land he might acquire. Just before sunrise, he was all set and went out with his servants, the chief and the other natives to earn his property. After they ascended a large hill overlooking the countryside, the chief waved his hand over everything within view. Pahom could hardly believe it, for the soil was thick and black, perfect for growing crops, as far as the eye could see. Ready to go, he left his money on the ground for the chief, took some provisions for himself and waited for the sun to peek over the horizon. As sunlight spilled over the land, Pahom set off to the east.

Every so often, to mark his territory, Pahom dug a hole with his spade and piled up turf. He went on for nearly three miles to the east and looked back; the people waiting for him to return seemed like ants on the hill. At noon, the heat oppressed him, so he stopped for lunch. The sun had grown hot so he pulled off his boots and took some time to drink water and rest. Then, he headed north onto the second leg of his journey.

Just when he thought about turning to the west, Pahom came upon an especially damp piece of land. *It would be a shame to leave this piece of land out*, he thought, so he continued farther north. After reaching the end of this damp stretch, he dug another hole and piled up the turf to mark the boundary, and headed west.

As he began the third leg of the trip, he could barely see the hill where he had started. Overcome with fatigue, he grew sleepy and languid. The sun continued to burn, and water did little to quench his thirst. Looking up, he saw that the sun was already halfway to the horizon. He was still far from reaching his goal. Thinking it best not to chance it, he headed directly toward the hill where his money waited.

On the final leg of the challenge, Pahom started to feel his knees give way as he jogged toward the hill. His feet were blistered and sweat cascaded down his face. *A few hours' pain for a lifetime of pleasure*, he thought.

As the hill finally became visible on the horizon, he feared that all was lost: He had gone too far and had made it too difficult to get back. He began to sprint, his heart hammering in his chest with every step. It was not until the sun had dipped halfway beneath the horizon that he could finally make out the people on the hill waving madly for him to return.

On and on he ran, and finally reached the foot of the hill; but as he did, his heart fell. The sun had disappeared. He had lost. But as he looked to the top of the hill, the people were still waving at him and yelling for him to continue. They were at the top of the hill and were higher than he was, so they could still see the sun! Pahom dashed up the hill, working his legs with every ounce of willpower available and dove toward the finish line, landing at his starting spot just as the sun was setting. The crowd burst out into praise.

"Ah, what a fine fellow!" exclaimed the chief. "He has gained much land!"

But when Pahom's servants turned toward their master, they found that Pahom had collapsed from the stress of the journey. When they checked on him, they realized he was dead.

Tolstoy concludes his story by stating that one of Pahom's servants picked up the spade Pahom had been using to plot his territory and dug a grave long enough for Pahom to be buried in. And the last line of Tolstoy's tale should convict us to the core, for it is a lesson in and of itself: "Six feet from his head to his heels was all he needed."[1]

How much land does a person need? Not much. Apparently, just six feet.

It seems that at the end of our lives, we aren't left with a whole lot. We can accumulate and store, and scrap and save, but one day we will lose all of it. Have you ever heard the saying, "You can't take it with you"? Paul wrote something similar to his disciple Timothy: "For we brought nothing into the world, and we can take nothing out of it" (1 Tim. 6:7).

Our lives can be much like Pahom's journey. On the first leg of our trip, we burst into the world with a youthful recklessness and high expectations. We're idealistic dreamers, aspiring for a happy and healthy life with a good amount of savings and a working car. We don't necessarily ask for much, just enough to get by.

On the second leg of our voyage, we become a bit wiser with experience and understand that with a little ingenuity and economic finesse, we can turn a small savings account into a sizeable retirement fund, a healthy money market account and maybe even grow a stock portfolio. We realize that the dreams we had as kids were not nearly large enough, or at least specific enough. Through hard work and some luck, we can make enough money to lead a comfortable life free from worry and live out the rest of our days in relative peace.

By the time we reach the third leg of life's journey, we've usually had some kind of setback. Maybe our stocks have plummeted or we get fired or we crash our car and watch the insurance skyrocket. There's always something that comes up, some unforeseen hiccup, and as we career past the middle of our lives toward the sunset years, we are forced to ask, "What have I accomplished in my lifetime? Have I done anything that matters?" We look back toward our starting point and wonder if we can make it back in time.

The fourth leg is a mad dash to the finish. From the outside, it won't look that way. It'll look like age and wrinkles and hospitals and sickness, but behind the tired eyes of the elderly—if you look closely enough—you can see the end rapidly approaching. Life is short, but it's even shorter when you've wasted most of it chasing after meaningless and unfulfilling desires. Some people will welcome the end of this race. Others will attempt to barter for more time.

But when we finally pass away, everything we have accumulated will go to someone else, whether they're a loved one (our spouse or children) or not (the government or a favorite charity). We will be forced to let go of our possessions as we cross over from earth to eternity. And the only thing we will take with us is the assurance that we can't bring anything material from this life into the next.

Though we're incapable of taking anything with us, it rarely stops us from trying. When the Greeks buried their dead, they placed two coins on the corpse's eyes so that when he traveled to the underworld, he would have something to pay the ferryman to carry him to the afterlife. The Egyptian pharaohs buried themselves with magnificent stores of gold because they believed they would need their wealth to survive in the afterlife. I once heard the story of a widow who placed two cans of spray adhesive into her husband's coffin because he used it to paste on his toupee. He was cremated, and when the fire reached the spray cans, they caused an explosion that bent the furnace door.[2] For some reason, these people believed they could transfer what they had accumulated from this life into the next one. Maybe we're the same way.

Just look around! Our lives are filled with all kinds of trinkets, talismans and treasures. Most of us own a mobile phone, a working car and, if we're fortunate, a house with a manageable mortgage or a decent rent. Of course, we need a refrigerator and a freezer and some food to fill it, a dinner table and silverware and plates and bowls and glasses. Definitely a bathroom with a working shower and hot, running water. We have that nice, flat-screen TV, and, in order to watch our favorite shows comfortably, we're going to need a couch on which to sit and a coffee table on which to kick up our feet. Then, some books to go on the coffee table so people will think we're studious, and a shelf to hold the other books we bought some time ago but never read. Naturally, we'll have to venture out of the house from time to time, so we'll need a closet full of fashionable clothes and a drawer full of exquisite accessories. But we don't "necessarily" have the cash up front to buy all of these "necessities," so we'll need some credit cards to shoulder the debt.

What's interesting to me is that many, if not most, middle-class Americans will think this is normal, but this mentality hardly represents the majority of people in the world. Did you know that the median income for a working person over the age of 25 in America is about $32,000?[3] That seems like a modest amount of income until you consider that the world's average income is closer to $7,000.[4] Most of what I mentioned earlier, the cars and the television sets and the furniture and the clothing and the books, are *luxuries* from the perspective of the average person in the world. Yet, we often assume that we need these things to survive.

Have you ever gone to your closet, looking through at least 10 outfits, and concluded that you had nothing to wear? Imagine owning only *one* set of clothing; that will quickly redefine how you look at your closet. My guess is that you could clear out your house and sell most of your things in a garage sale or on Craigslist.org and still have plenty left over.

Now, before you start chucking your possessions onto the street, I must mention that having wealth is not a bad thing. In fact, we can use our material possessions to propel the mission of God's kingdom here on earth. The problem arises when we regard our luxuries as *necessities*. They are not necessities; we just think they are. We don't gather possessions religiously because we actually *need* them; most often, we collect them because they make us feel successful, comfortable, safe.

But here's my question: At the end of our lives, what do we have left? When all is said and done, and we're standing in the full radiance of the Lord's majesty and glory, what have we accomplished that has true worth or value in eternity?

John Piper, in his book *Don't Waste Your Life*, tells a story his father often shared from the pulpit concerning an elderly man who had continually refused the Christian life. The church had not given up on this unbeliever, praying for him through the decades of his life; but he was bitter and stubborn. He simply refused to believe. That's why it was such a shock when the man entered the church's sanctuary during one of the elder Piper's sermons. What's more, the old man walked down the aisle during the hymn of invitation! After the church was dismissed, Piper's father sat him down in the front pew and shared the gospel message that Jesus had died for this man and was offering grace and salvation. The old man accepted Jesus into his heart that very day, but the joy he felt from his decision did not stop him from weeping. As tears streamed down his face, the old man cried, "I've wasted it! I've wasted it!"[5]

The rest of this chapter is for those of you who don't want to reflect back over your life and feel as if you've wasted it. It is for those who want something better than simply making plans to acquire earthly treasure. James addresses this very topic in James 4:13-17 of his epistle:

> Now listen, you who say, "Today or tomorrow we will go to this or that city, spend a year there, carry on business and make money." Why, you do not even know what will happen tomorrow. What is your life? You are a mist that appears for a little while and then vanishes. Instead, you ought to say, "If it is the Lord's will, we will live and do this or that." As it is, you boast in your arrogant schemes. All such boasting is evil. If anyone, then, knows the good they ought to do and doesn't do it, it is sin for them.

The problem that James highlights is people who make plans without understanding life's brevity, and without submitting to God's sovereignty. Within this earnest text, God offers an app to anyone who feels like there is something more to life—that there's something more than what we can see with our eyes and grasp with our hands. It is a spiritual accounting program that will show you how to invest your wealth, your time, your energy, your relationships and everything else you have in this life into a retirement fund of unlimited worth, a fund that can never be emptied. We'll download this app in six steps.

## Step 1: Track Your Spending

In the Scripture text you just read, James described a situation in which a person, probably a merchant or trader, says to someone, "Look. I've got this great business plan, and I want to make you a partner. I've found this woman in Jerusalem who spins the most beautiful garments. Seriously, the material feels like Egyptian cotton. But she's got no panache when it comes to business. I mean she's selling a square cubit for a shekel. She's practically giving it away for free! So here's my idea: We contract her to spin a huge bulk of garment—I'm thinking at least 100 square cubits—then we cart it off to Jericho and spend a year selling the stuff. Of course, we'll weight the scales a little in our favor, maybe dodge the taxes by paying off the tax collector. Once we have a cash base, we can invest in landownership, build our clientele, move to Caesarea and live like kings. Whaddya say?" (I've used poetic license with the text here, as we don't know what conversations actually took place, but you get the gist.)

When we downloaded God's app to resuscitate a dying faith in chapter 4, we saw that in the economy in Judea and the surrounding Roman world, most people were either aristocrats who controlled the income or peasants who worked hard labor. There were, however, people who neither slaved in the fields nor owned property. The majority of these people were merchants—men and women who would buy from someone wholesale and sell to another at a higher price in order to make a profit. They were vendors, the middlemen between the artisans and the buyers.[6]

James is addressing these specific kinds of people, those who make plans to go to this or that city and sell this or that item for such and such a price. But what is so wrong with what they're doing? Is he disapproving of all merchants? Does James's command mean that we should immediately quit our jobs in retail and sales?

Of course not. James's problem with these believers goes much deeper. For one, their plans are completely bankrupt of anything remotely spiritual. They want to take a year to travel abroad and make money. That's fine, but what about the fact that there are people in this world who do not yet know the message of the gospel? What about those who have no food to eat? What about those children who are wandering the streets homeless and without parents? What about those who are sick and in need of healing? Can they casually live out their lives without concern over the many who are lost or broken?

The merchants betray their priorities from the get-go. Their prime concern is making a profit. And the problem is not that they want to pocket some cash but that fulfilling these profitable plans is their *primary* goal.

This is why they get up in the morning—to make money. And the question is: Why spend an entire year for the sole purpose of gaining something you cannot keep? In 1 Timothy 6:9-10, Paul shares the following insight with his disciple Timothy:

> People who want to get rich fall into temptation and a trap and into many foolish and harmful desires that plunge men into ruin and destruction. For the love of money is a root of all kinds of evil. Some people, eager for money, have wandered from the faith and pierced themselves with many griefs.

Paul calls the pursuit of money a trap, and in my opinion, it's one of those traps that has spikes at the bottom.

So how do you avoid this trap? The answer lies in identifying those priorities that are taking the majority of your time, which leads to our first step toward prioritizing our investments: track your spending. Find out where you're spending your money, time and energy, and you'll quickly discover your priorities. Keep a vigilant eye on your checkbook. Pay attention to your budget. Chart how you're spending your time throughout the day. Record your conversations and notice when you're engaged and when you're disinterested.

You may be surprised at what you find. For instance, how much more time did you spend watching television than in prayer? Have you invested more money in department stores like Nordstrom and Macy's than in the church? When you are exhausted at the end of the day, is it because you work for something temporary or eternal? Are you more excited when you talk about sports or movies than when you talk about your faith?

These are only a few questions and methods for uncovering what you have deemed to be essential in your life. Once you've properly tracked them, it's your responsibility to begin unearthing them. In doing so, you will achieve the first step in God's app to prioritize your investments.

**DOWNLOAD IN PROGRESS**

■■■■■■■■■■■▪▫▫▫▫▫▫▫▫▫▫▫▫▫▫▫▫▫▫▫▫▫▫▫▫▫▫▫▫▫▫▫▫▫▫▫▫▫▫▫▫▫

0%      10%      20%      30%    40%    50%    60%    70%    80%    90%

## Step 2: Unearth Those Idols

In his book *Counterfeit Gods*, Timothy Keller writes about the tragic string of suicides committed by formerly wealthy and well-connected individuals in the world of finance after the economic downfall in mid-2008. The chief financial officer of the home financing group Freddie Mac hanged himself in his basement. The chief executive of Sheldon Good, a U.S. real estate auction firm, shot himself in the head behind the wheel of his red Jaguar. A Bear Stearns executive overdosed on drugs and jumped from the twenty-ninth floor of his office building when he discovered that JP Morgan Chase, who had bought his firm, wouldn't bring him along.[7]

These are extreme examples, but they show us the kind of devotion with which we're dealing. They also teach us a vital lesson: Whatever we prioritize is what we idolize. Consider this quote from Keller:

> As a pastor I've had people come to me to confess that they struggle with almost every kind of sin. Almost. I cannot

recall anyone ever coming to me and saying, "I spend too much money on myself. I think my greedy lust for money is harming my family, my soul, and people around me." Greed hides itself from the victim. The money god's modus operandi includes blindness to your own heart.[8]

The dramatic ways in which these top executives took their lives illustrates the destination to which a life in the unchecked pursuit of wealth leads and also shows us the depths to which greed can penetrate the human heart and control the human will.

I am reminded of a story about Jacob, recorded in Genesis 31:19-37. After marrying both daughters of a certain man named Laban, the younger daughter, Rachel, stole Laban's "household gods." They were idols, most likely either stone or wooden figurines, which Laban kept in his house as a means of protection and divine aid. Like many others in that time, Laban believed that these "gods" were responsible for making it rain or causing the sun to shine or allowing crops to grow. Men like Laban would pray to these gods in order to remain in their favor.

Jacob's wife Rachel also believed that these idols had supernatural powers, so she stole them in an effort to gain the gods' favor for Jacob and his family. When Laban realized that his idols were gone, he pursued Jacob, thinking that he had stolen them. When Laban finally caught up to Jacob, he searched everywhere among his tents and caravan, making a fuss as he went on about the importance of these idols. But Rachel hid them in her camel's saddle and sat on them to hide them.

By now, you may be thinking, *How strange! Why were these people so concerned with a few figurines, especially since they only represented figments of their imagination?* In short, it was because these were the objects of their *worship*.

Laban's and Rachel's actions expose an unholy obsession and an unworthy priority. They show that people will do absolutely anything for the object of their worship—i.e., betray and steal from one's own father or behave like a lunatic by ransacking the home of one's son-in-law. Whatever we have prioritized as our primary concern is what we worship. It doesn't just have to be wealth—it could be anything ranging from a sports team, movie star or music icon, to a hobby or even your own family or friends. Anything that takes precedence over God becomes an idol.

Recently, I heard about a fan of University of Alabama's football team who decided to show his devotion by claiming to have poisoned the historic trees on the campus of the University of Auburn, which is a big rival of Alabama. As I listened to him explain his actions on the radio, he sounded sincerely deranged. After all, he named his two children Crimson Tyde [sic], after Alabama's varsity teams, and Bear Bryant, after Alabama's revered football coach. Some might regard this man as insane, and that may be true, but he also represents someone who is clearly devoted to his first love.[9]

We act in similar ways, even if we do it on a much smaller scale. The merchants in James 4 turned their business enterprise into an idol, and for that, James was forced to plead with them to unearth those unholy obsessions and unworthy priorities. He pleads with us today to bring out any and all of *our* idols from hiding and allow Christ to begin to work in our hearts anew. May He begin that work in us today.

**DOWNLOAD IN PROGRESS**

| 0% | 10% | 20% | 30% | 40% | 50% | 60% | 70% | 80% | 90% |

## Step 3: Remember the Epitaph

The third step toward reprioritizing our investments is to realize that every material thing in this world has a shelf life. Clothing loses its color and eventually tears or rips; moths creep in and nibble away. Food spoils and rots. Buildings erode. Stocks fluctuate and plummet. Smartphones and laptop computers will crash or get hacked or become outdated. Houses get robbed. Money loses its value.

Eventually, we too will fade away.

We know this, and yet for some reason we never take this fundamental truth seriously. Very few of us live as though we might suddenly pass away, as though we might not see tomorrow. Often, we take for granted the time we have been given.

James has a response for this attitude:

Why, you do not even know what will happen tomorrow. What is your life? You are a mist that appears for a little while and then vanishes (4:14).

Here, James identifies a problem that is much deeper than greed. He's talking about mortality, and for James, the two ideas are linked in an incredibly important way.

Bragging about one's plans for the future is silly for two reasons: (1) a life in the pursuit of money is futile and fruitless, (2) because it focuses on goods that only exist for a very short time when compared to what lasts for eternity. The merchants' future plans are really not future plans at all, because tomorrow is never guaranteed. They boast about tomorrow, confident that they will be alive and well, as if circumstances affecting their plans will not change, and as if Christ Himself would not return. They are making plans as if they are immortal; but at this point, none of us are.

Death sometimes comes at the most unexpected of times. On March 3, 2011, ESPN ran the story of Wes Leonard, a junior basketball player for Fennville High School, Fennville, Michigan, who after making the winning shot to protect his team's undefeated season suddenly collapsed on the floor and passed away. Many who knew him came forward and described him as a great kid, a highly skilled athlete and a humble student. His superintendent dubbed him "the quintessential all-American kid," and his coach said that Wes was special because he could see the "big picture" and that "he takes care of his body better than probably anybody I've ever coached." This boy was the picture of health, and yet in his moment of greatest triumph, and during probably one of the best moments of his life, he died. Just like that.[10]

I think about that story and realize that life could end at any time. A few years ago at our church, I began a message series that was a study through the book of James. The week before I preached on this very text in James, my father went into the doctor's office for some tests. As my father was leaving his physician's office after his appointment, the doctor asked, "You're feeling okay, right?"

My father responded, "Yeah, I'm good. I'm a little tired sometimes."

The doctor motioned for my dad to sit back down, talked a little more, ran a few more tests and found out that the main artery running to his heart was 95 percent clogged. About 40 percent of his heart wasn't getting any oxygen.

In a way, we're all just a moment away from a heart attack or a brain aneurysm or a stroke or an auto accident. Every time we slide our key into the ignition of our car and drive out onto the road, we are taking a chance that we might not get to our destination alive. There are no guarantees concerning how long we get to live here on earth. We are all just a heartbeat away—one small breath—from eternity.

For some, that might be a paralyzing thought; but for me, that notion drives me to accomplish as much as possible right now while I'm still drawing breath. When I die, I want the epitaph on my gravestone to tell the truth about the kind of life I've lived. In a sense, I'm always remembering my epitaph, because I know I could pass at any moment.

I once read that Philip of Macedon, the father of Alexander the Great, appointed a servant to visit him every day and say to him, "Philip, you will die."[11] He did this because he understood that the prospect of death should change the outcome of the way we live. I've spoken to people who have had close scrapes with death, either a car accident or an injury or a disease, and as you would expect, their lives completely changed. Their priorities shifted, their goals became much more focused, they procrastinated less and loved more. Since brushing against death, their entire outlook has changed. The time they once took for granted has now become a precious commodity.

This is what James is attempting to teach us in this short text. With an eye on our epitaph, we will begin to live as if every day was our last on this earth.

**DOWNLOAD IN PROGRESS**

| 0% | 10% | 20% | 30% | 40% | 50% | 60% | 70% | 80% | 90% |

## Step 4: Set the Camera to Panorama

Our lives in the scope of eternity are like a tenth of a second, so little time that you barely notice it. The good news is that there's actually a lot you can do in a tenth of a second. Just ask David Lee. On December 20, 2006, the New York Knicks were playing basketball at home against the Charlotte Bobcats. The game went to double-overtime. Both sides of the court were weary from the contest but both kept fighting for the win.

The score was tied at 109, and the Knicks had the ball with 0.1 seconds left in the game. Technically, you can't score in 0.1 seconds. According to the Trent Tucker rule, you need at least 0.3 seconds to catch and release a shot before the buzzer. Otherwise, it's ruled "no good." It looked like the Knicks and the Bobcats were heading into a third overtime. But as the Knicks inbounded the ball from the sideline, they threw it directly toward the hoop, and David Lee leapt into the air, barely brushed the ball and tipped it into the hoop. Madison Square Garden erupted in cheers. The officials ruled that the shot was good. The Knicks won 111-109 on a play that lasted 0.1 seconds.[12]

A tenth of a second could be the difference between winning and losing. It matters, even in the scope of eternity. Our lives matter, no matter how short, especially when they are spent in service to others.

When James rebukes the merchants for their financial endeavors, at the deepest level he is exposing their selfishness; they're only thinking of themselves. Instead of placing confidence in their economic prowess, James challenges them in 4:15, stating, "You ought to say, 'If it is the Lord's will, we will live and do this or that.'"

This is the solution to the problem. One phrase, six words. "If it is the Lord's will." If we started our sentences with those six words, everything about our lives would change.

Seriously, *everything* would change, and not just from saying those words out loud. It's not a slogan; it's an entire way of viewing life. When we live by "If it is the Lord's will," the way that we see the world completely changes. Harry Emerson Fosdick likens this concept to a person who lives in a room full of mirrors. Every way he turns, he only sees himself. But when he forgets himself, the mirrors in his room turn into windows. He no longer sees himself; he sees out into the world beyond and becomes aware of what needs to be done.[13]

The undercurrent to everything James has been saying in these few verses—the reason why pursuing wealth is foolish and why focusing on earthly matters is futile—is because we're part of something much, much bigger than ourselves. Paul declares in Ephesians 6:12, "For our struggle is not against flesh and blood, but against the rulers, against the authorities, against the powers of this dark world and against the spiritual forces of evil in the heavenly realms." In other words, a battle is being fought over the fate of humankind, and quite frankly, we do not have time to waste. How can we spend it concentrating on ourselves when there are billions of people on this earth who do not yet know Christ?

There is a larger picture here. In God's sovereignty, He calls on us to impact the world. So when we say, "If it is the Lord's will," we are asking, "Will my plans factor into God's plan to touch the world?" Wherever you go to work or wherever you sit in class or whenever you visit your family or hang out with your friends, ask yourself if what you are doing here and now is part of God's plan for redeeming mankind from sin. Hebrews 10:35-37 inspires us in this manner: "Do not throw away your confidence; it will be richly rewarded. You need to persevere so that when you have done the will of God, you will receive what he has promised. For, 'In just a little while, he who is coming will come and will not delay.' "

God has been accomplishing His will for some time now, and this is the main reason why we submit to His will. He sees the whole picture in panorama while we only catch snippets. Like a general on a hill overlooking his armies, the Lord can see the entire battlefield and has developed the strategy to win. A soldier on the frontlines does not control the army, because he cannot see the wider threat, but only what's in front of him. It's the same with us. We can only see our small corner of the world; we are not able to comprehend how the Lord is impacting the entire world, not just today but throughout all of history.

The important step for us, then, is to realize that we're living with blinders on, staring down the scope of our lives in tunnel vision. In order to prioritize our investments, we must place our trust in the God who sees the entire picture. We must be willing to surrender ourselves to Him so that He can use us to accomplish His perfect and glorious will, now and for eternity.

## Step 5: Envision the Invisible

There was once an old clockmaker who was nearing the end of his life. As he lay on his deathbed, his three children began to talk among themselves. Of course, they were sad for their father's illness, but they were also somewhat excited, for they believed their father to be a wildly rich man. After all, his clocks were of the finest quality, displayed in some of the most prestigious locales on the earth. Some had even sworn to seeing movie actors and famous politicians entering his store and purchasing his creations.

The clockmaker, knowing that he was nearing death, asked for his will, and when they brought it to him, he cleared his throat and read it before his children.

"To my eldest son," he said. "I leave my work." His eldest son beamed, for he had been training under his father and understood that his father would leave him the shop.

"To my youngest son, I leave my trust." The youngest son was overjoyed, for he knew that his father had developed a substantial trust fund over the years.

"And to my only daughter, I leave my love." She blushed. Of course, he meant his prize piece, a grandfather clock standing at 12 feet, inlaid with gold and silver and constructed from Brazilian Rosewood. It was rumored that the bells that chimed within the clock were obtained from the private stores of the king of Syria some 200 years ago. He had spent 10 years of his life constructing this wonder, and its worth was regarded as inestimable.

The clockmaker coughed. "I know it isn't much," he said, "but I give it to you."

"Not much?" the children exclaimed. "To leave us your most prized possessions, your shop, your savings and your prized clock is to leave us with more than enough. You are a good father, generous to us with your wealth."

Their father looked confused. "But that is not what I left for you. The shop has been sold, along with the grandfather clock, and I have very little in savings."

His children were stunned. "You cannot be serious," his eldest son said. "You sold the shop and the clock and have nothing left?"

"I sold the shop and the clock for what I thought it was worth. Of course, you will receive that as well, although it isn't much at all."

His children began to weep. He had left them with nothing.

Their father was surprised. "Do not weep," he said, "as if I have left you with nothing. For I *have* given you my most prized possessions. To my eldest son, I give my work, the desire to strive your entire life and labor as if your life depended on it, and to ask for little in return. To my youngest son, my trust, for throughout my life, my friends and neighbors knew that I was not a proud or greedy man and would never seek to extort them. And to my only daughter, I give my love, for I see that same compassion bursting from her heart as I have striven to sustain in mine. I have given you what I prized above all things, the things that will last beyond me and beyond you and beyond your children. What else did you expect?"

We need to take a look at our own hearts. What do we expect in this life from our Father? Trust funds, shops and grandfather clocks that will only fade away in time? Material goods that will eventually rust or deteriorate or get lost in the shuffle? Or should we expect something more, something of much more value?

Notice what 2 Corinthians 4:18 says: "So we [believers] fix our eyes not on what is seen, but on what is unseen, since what is seen is temporary, but what is unseen is eternal." The difference is with our focus. Are we focused on temporary or eternal matters?

Jesus said, "I tell you, use worldly wealth to gain friends for yourselves, so that when it is gone, you will be welcomed into eternal dwellings" (Luke 16:9). The job to which we go every day is no longer a place just to make money. Instead, it becomes a place to encounter people who haven't met Christ; it becomes an opportunity to exemplify the character of Christ through hard work and integrity and earns us enough extra money to help feed and clothe those who have nothing. Our bank accounts are transformed into funding centers for missionary work or poverty alleviation. Our cars become vehicles for the gospel message. Our homes become places to show Christ's hospitality to those whom others wouldn't invite.

This download step compels us to reprioritize our lives as we learn to envision the invisible. God is calling us to see the world with new eyes, and He is asking us to see the eternal potential in all that we do and accomplish here on earth.

**DOWNLOAD IN PROGRESS**

0% 10% 20% 30% 40% 50% 60% 70% 80% 90%

## Step 6: Invest in a Better Retirement Community

The final step of our app is found in the pivotal words Jesus spoke during His illustrious Sermon on the Mount. He said, "Do not store up for yourselves treasures on earth, where moths and vermin destroy, and where thieves break in and steal. But store up for yourselves treasures in heaven, where moth and vermin do not destroy, and where thieves do not break in and steal. For where your treasure is, there your heart will be also" (Matt. 6:19-21).

Jesus' words highlight the reality that no matter how much we accumulate in this life, it will be mere pennies compared to what the Lord has in store for us in heaven. To worry about or pursue earthly treasure is like an oil tycoon arguing over wooden nickels. There is a greater inheritance waiting for us, and in the scope of eternity, we really don't have to wait that long for it.

I love the story of William Borden, a brilliant young seminary student who, in 1913, moved to Cairo in order to learn Arabic. He was planning to become a missionary to the Muslim population and he had worked diligently for years learning how to study the Scriptures. Mastering this new language was the final step of his preparation before entering the mission field full-time. However, during his stay in Cairo, he contracted malaria and died. Despite all of his preparation and hard work, all of the years he poured into his goal, he never made it to the mission field. In the leaf of his Bible, the following words were inscribed:

*No reserves, no retreats, no regrets.*

Many would consider William Borden's life a failure, but he certainly didn't. Though he never got to achieve his dream of serving as missionary to Cairo, he did not regret his untimely death, for he understood that an eternity of glory awaited him.[14] The apostle Paul understood this as well when he wrote in Philippians 1:21: "For to me, to live is Christ and to die is gain." Both of these godly servants realized there was not only value in this world but also in the world to come.

Thus, the final step to downloading God's app to reprioritize your investments is to look heavenward and know that all of the frustrations you might endure as you attempt to love and serve others is being converted into a heavenly investment. In fact, this download begins and ends with the reality of heaven. When Jesus was teaching His disciples to pray, He instructed them to say, "Our Father in heaven, hallowed be your name, your kingdom come, your will be done, on earth as it is in heaven" (Matt. 6:9-10).

Your prayer and mine should always be that the Father's will be done "on earth as it is in heaven." Every time we choose to do the Father's will, we are, in a sense, bringing heaven to earth. When you reach out to a friend who is struggling with addiction and offer healing or assistance, you're bringing heaven to earth. If you see someone in need and offer food or clothing or shelter, you're taking part in heaven's collision with earth. When we reconcile embittered enemies toward one another or counsel husbands and wives to restore broken homes, we are ushering in God's kingdom on earth and helping hasten the time when God will make eternal peace by uniting heaven and earth under His reign.

Everything we've incorporated into our lives from this chapter has been aimed at becoming followers of Christ who are determined to accomplish their Father's will as they head toward the heavenly gates. It is all about heaven, and even more than that, doing the will of the Father on earth—just as it is being done in heaven.

**DOWNLOAD COMPLETE!**

In this chapter, you have discovered six steps toward downloading God's app for prioritizing your investments:

- Keep track of your spending (money, time, energy, relationships). In this way, you can quickly discover whatever has supplanted God's role as the number-one priority in your life.
- Realize that any priority that trumps God's position in your life has become an idol. You must unearth those idols and expose them to the light of Christ before they consume you.
- Live so that the words on your epitaph inspire generations to come. You will pass away someday, and you only have one chance in this life to make an impact for the kingdom of God.
- Keep in mind that you are part of a much grander story. We seek to accomplish the Lord's will because He is the One who sees everything and who possesses the best strategy to save the world.
- Learn to see the invisible qualities in this world (love and compassion), which will help you refocus on matters of eternal significance.

- Store up treasures in heaven. By seeking to accomplish
  the previous five steps, you open an account in a trust
  fund that will never empty.

Dear friend, remember that your investments on earth are
temporary, but your investments in heaven are forever. They will
never spoil, fade or disappear. James urges us to forget about ourselves and focus wholly on accomplishing God's will, setting our
eyes toward heaven. For in the blink of an eye, we will never again
see this decaying world and its crumbling attractions . . . but only
see the Father's purposes for this world, His mission to save it, and
eternity bursting over the horizon.

## God Has an App to
# Heal Your Affliction

### James 5:1-19

Thirteen surgeries is a staggering number of medical procedures in one's lifetime, especially considering that Hailey Garland is only 15 years old. Born with neurofibromatosis, a genetically inherited disorder in which the nerve tissue grows tumors throughout the body, this young girl has already had one surgery on her brain, four on her back, four on her throat, and three on her stomach. She has two titanium rods in her spine, with 55 screws.

Most recently, Hailey went to the hospital because she couldn't hear out of her right ear or feel the entire right side of her body. Her doctors think that these symptoms could be the result of tumors pressing on her spinal cord and causing acute dizziness and numbness. Barring a divine miracle, Hailey will most likely have to endure many more hospital visits and tests as her physicians diligently work to keep the tumors at bay. It is tough to fathom how someone could be so familiar with affliction at such a young age.

*Affliction* is defined as "a state of misery, distress, or grief; a cause of mental or bodily pain, as in sickness, loss, calamity, or persecution."[1] Like the stress and temptation we examined in chapters 1 and 2, affliction also carries an element of inevitability for every person, due to the dark and fallen state of the world in which we live. You see, when God created the first man and woman, whose story is recorded in Genesis 2, He provided everything for them so that they might live in a peaceful paradise and enjoy walking with Him daily. But after Adam and Eve rebelled against God, the earth was placed under a curse (see Gen. 3:17). Disease and death rode in on the coattails of iniquity, and we live under this curse to this day.

However, we understand from Scriptures like Galatians 3:13 and Revelation 22:3 that God has provided us with ultimate victory and salvation, and that one day we will be with Him forever in heaven. In the meantime, the devil is being permitted rule in our present world to a certain degree (see John 12:31; 14:30; 2 Cor. 4:4; Eph. 2:2). Our enemy, the afflicter, desires to use pain and suffering to drive a wedge between God and His beloved children, for our human tendency is to reject or blame the Lord in times of great hardship. But as believers walking in the light and piercing the surrounding darkness, we must understand the spiritual nature of our present afflictions and know that He who is in us is greater than he who is in the world (see 1 John 4:4).

God, who lives in our hearts, is in the business of healing. In fact, His ability and willingness to heal us physically and spiritually are important facets of His marvelous character and His awesome name! In Exodus 15:22-26, God identifies Himself to the people of Israel as Yahweh-Rophe for the first time. This name literally means "God is healer" or "God who heals." After Moses led the Israelites from the Red Sea and into the Desert of Shur, they traveled for three days in the arid land without finding water. When they came to a place called Marah, they couldn't drink its water because it was bitter, so the people began to grumble against their leader. Then Moses cried out to God, and God performed a great miracle: He showed Moses a piece of wood and instructed him to throw it into the water. When Moses did so, the water suddenly became as pure as mountain spring water delivered straight to your door!

Then, God gave Moses and the Israelites the following promise:

He said, "If you listen carefully to the LORD your God and do what is right in his eyes, if you pay attention to his commands and keep all his decrees, I will not bring on you any of the diseases I brought on the Egyptians, for I am the LORD, who heals you" (Exod. 15:26).

This passage in Exodus is the only time Yahweh-Rophe appears in the Word of God, but our heavenly Father's power to heal is further reinforced throughout the Old Testament (see 2 Kings 20:1-11; Ps. 103:1-45) and, of course, by the many who were healed miraculously by Jesus and His disciples in the New Testament (see Matt. 8 and 9 for just a few examples). This healing is not limited to the pages of our Bible. God still heals! His nature and character are eternal; He is "the same yesterday and today and forever" (Heb. 13:8).

Furthermore, we know that "God is love" (1 John 4:16) and that He desires to give abundant life (see John 10:10) and good gifts to His children (see Jas. 1:5,17). We can deduce from these Scriptures, and many others to follow, that being healed from our present infirmities is a part of the blessing the Lord desires to bestow upon us. And while you and I may not understand why He chooses to heal in some situations and not in others, we can trust that God—who did not spare even His own Son so that we could have eternal life—always has our best interests at heart.

But if you have stood helplessly beside a loved one who passed away without any sudden healing; if you've been struggling with an illness yourself; or if you've observed seemingly strange televangelists performing faith healings on TV, I know you may be cynical toward the idea that God really does heal people. My hope is that, by fully downloading God's app to heal your affliction, certain myths or misconceptions you may be harboring will be set straight as you glean a deeper understanding of what the Bible says about healing. Of course, I will not be able to encapsulate the entirety of this heavy topic within one chapter; however, I would highly recommend a book by a dear friend of mine, Dr. Jim Garlow. He has studied the topic of healing extensively and is intimately familiar with affliction, as his wife, Carol, has been fighting a tenacious battle with cancer. Together they have written a book called *God Still Heals: Answers to Your Questions About Divine Healing*, and I quote this wonderful book within step three of this app.

We will begin our download shortly, but first, it's important to identify the two types of affliction James discusses in the fifth chapter of his epistle. At some point or another, we will all need healing, either physically or spiritually. And since each causes suffering, heartache and pain, let's take a closer look at these two categories of affliction before we dive into God's healing app.

## Physical Affliction

After years of begging and pleading, my oldest daughter, Kayla, finally talked my wife and me into letting her have a Boxer puppy. At the time, Kayla was in college studying kinesiology, the study of human movement. The university she attended had a nationally respected, state-of-the-art facility for adaptive therapeutic exercise, which was geared toward people with extreme disabilities to enable them to improve or maintain their health as best as possible. Kayla was truly moved by some of the people with whom she worked and the difficult injuries and illnesses they faced.

As she sought a name for her new puppy, Kayla desired something unique that would give her an opportunity to share an uplifting story to her clients who were often desperately ill. There are a number of stories of sickness recorded in the Bible, but she was drawn to the story of King Hezekiah, the legendary king of Judah, of whom 2 Kings 18:5 says, "There was no one like him among all the kings of Judah, either before him or after him." The Scriptures tells us that King Hezekiah trusted in the Lord; in fact, his very name means "God is my strength."

But one day, Hezekiah became deathly ill and was advised to begin making funeral preparations. The king cried out to the Lord, saying, "Remember, LORD, how I have walked before you faithfully and with wholehearted devotion and have done what is good in your eyes" (2 Kings 20:3). Because of Hezekiah's plea and his righteous walk before the Lord, his prayer was heard and God healed him from his illness (see 2 Kings 20:5-6).

This story resonated in my daughter's heart, and—as you may have already guessed—she decided to name her puppy "Hezekiah," or

"Kiah" for short. Of course, whenever Kayla would tell people her dog's name, they would inevitably ask where such an unusual name came from. She would then share how God miraculously and mercifully healed King Hezekiah, which offered hope to those who were suffering.

Hezekiah's story draws our attention to the fact that every person in the world is subject to physical affliction; no one is immune—not even a faithful, God-fearing king. Disease and the deterioration of our earthly bodies are inescapable; just take a look at these findings from a recent National Health Interview Survey in which close to 28,000 American adults were surveyed:

- 12 percent of all adults had been told they had heart disease.
- 24 percent had been diagnosed with hypertension.
- 13 percent had asthma.
- 8 percent had faced cancer.
- 9 percent had dealt with diabetes.
- 22 percent had some form of arthritis.
- 28 percent had shown chronic joint pain symptoms.
- 16 percent had experienced a migraine or severe headache within three months of the interview.
- 28 percent suffered from low back pain.
- 15 percent had difficulty hearing.
- 8 percent had struggled with poor vision.[2]

While sickness in some form or another is unavoidable, King Hezekiah's story also directs us to an important reality: There is a loving Creator, the Author of Life, Yahweh-Rophe, "God who heals," who hears our cry and is able to restore our physical health. And just as He is able to heal us physically, God is also able to heal us spiritually.

## Spiritual Affliction

"What's wrong, honey?" I asked my wife, Renee, who had just gotten home from church. Right away I noticed her petite body quivering, and the look of concern on her face.

"Dudley," she said, "today in church, I had my eyes closed while I was singing and worshiping the Lord, and when I opened my eyes I saw the most alarming thing."

I was very intrigued at this point, and asked, "What was it?"

"Well, there was a man with a shaved head standing in the row in front of me. His back was toward me, and he had this huge mole on the back of his head."

I guess moles can be weird enough, but I didn't understand why it bothered my wife so much until she continued, "That wasn't the scary part," she said. "The man had a tattoo around the mole. The tattoo was a picture of this fierce-looking face, and the big mole was the pupil of one of the eyes of the face!" (To see a photo of the tattoo, visit www.GodHasAnApp.com.)

"Whoa!" I said.

"I know!" Renee replied. "It's difficult to worship when you've got this frightening tattoo staring back at you, with a mole in the center. But then I took my focus off the tattoo and saw that the man's arms were raised as he sang freely to the Lord. All of his children were standing next to him, and their arms were raised too. Dudley, it was such a precious sight to see all of them there just praising God together."

Tears welled up in Renee's eyes as she finished her story. Meanwhile, I was thinking about how I could find this guy so I could see his crazy tattoo! It didn't take me long to discover that the man, Ruben, was an active member of one of our men's ministries. But he hadn't always been such a devoted parishioner in the church. You see, before Ruben became a Christian, he had lived a hard life and actually battled cancer for several years. I learned that his entire family, including his children, began to pray for him fervently—not that he would be healed from cancer, but that he would be saved. God, in His great and awesome mercy, did both!

While Ruben happened to be suffering from the physical kind of affliction, his family recognized that there was much more at stake: his spiritual wellbeing. Therefore, they prayed that he would accept Jesus Christ as his Lord and Savior, for the forgiveness of his sins. They wanted Ruben to experience peace with God and everlasting life in heaven.

Sin, which is a rebellion against and a rejection of God, separates us from having a relationship with the Lord and is the source of our spiritual affliction. It is an invisible disease that infiltrates the heart of every person who doesn't know Jesus Christ, "for there is no other name under heaven given to mankind by which we must be saved" (Acts 4:12). We are healed spiritually, just as Ruben was, when we put our trust in Jesus Christ, for Romans 3:23-24 says that "all have sinned and fall short of the glory of God, and all are justified freely by his grace through the redemption that came by Christ Jesus."

I want to highlight the word "justified" here. What this means is that through our faith in Jesus, we are suddenly "made right" in God's eyes; we are healed of the spiritual disease that formerly plagued us! So while being healed of physical ailments is possible through God's power and grace, what is paramount is when you and I are healed of our spiritual illness.

After we become Christians, this kind of affliction can rear its ugly head in the form of unforgiveness, bitterness, lying, cheating, stealing, lust, pride and other sins. We sometimes fall back into the old transgressions we dabbled in before we became saved, and this is quite debilitating to an upright Christian walk. For this reason, just as Ruben was healed both physically and spiritually, God's app to heal your affliction will address both types of affliction. By thoroughly examining James 5:13-18, you will learn how to experience the freedom of a healthy life in Christ. Let's start the download!

**BEGIN DOWNLOAD**

| 0% | 10% | 20% | 30% | 40% | 50% | 60% | 70% | 80% | 90% |

## Step 1: Get Season Tickets

Here's a bit of trivia for you: Any idea what song holds the record for the number-one tune with the oldest lyrics on the *Billboard* charts? In 1959, American folk singer Pete Seeger adapted a song entirely from chapter 3 of the book of Ecclesiastes in the Bible (with the exception of the last line) and recorded it in 1962. The song is entitled, "Turn! Turn! Turn! (To Everything There Is a Season)." It became an international hit in late 1965, when it was covered by The Byrds and reached #1 on the *Billboard* Hot 100 chart.

Though the sequence of the words was rearranged for the song, the lyrics are taken almost verbatim from Ecclesiastes 3:1-8, which was written by Solomon:

> There is a time for everything,
> and a season for every activity under the heavens:
> a time to be born and a time to die,
> a time to plant and a time to uproot,
> a time to kill and a time to heal,
> a time to tear down and a time to build,
> a time to weep and a time to laugh,
> a time to mourn and a time to dance,
> a time to scatter stones and a time to gather them,
> a time to embrace and a time to refrain from embracing,
> a time to search and a time to give up,
> a time to keep and a time to throw away,
> a time to tear and a time to mend,
> a time to be silent and a time to speak,
> a time to love and a time to hate,
> a time for war and a time for peace.

These words of wisdom are closely related to the first step to God's app to heal your affliction, which is to accept the fact that there indeed is a season for everything.

James 5:13 reads, "Is anyone among you in trouble? Let them pray. Is anyone happy? Let them sing songs of praise." One moment, you can be driving on the freeway, belting out the worship song "Shout to the Lord," because you just got a promotion, your family is healthy, your favorite sports team is on a winning streak and you are having a fabulous hair day. It is quite natural to sing praises to God when you're happy. But it's amazing how quickly circumstances can turn sour. While checking out your fabulous hair in the rearview mirror, you suddenly rear-end the driver in front of you. Then you are notified that the company you work for is going to have to lay off several people and you might be one of them. What's worse, you get a call from the doctor with discouraging news about your ailing parent or grandparent, or test results of your own. As natural as it is to sing "Hallelujah!" to the Lord when times are good, it is equally natural to cry out to Him when trouble comes.

In life, there is truly a season for everything—famine and feast, war and peace, cheerfulness and great sorrow. James's second encouragement to us in chapter 5 verse 13 is to do what is appropriate in each season. Recently, an 85-year-old Catholic nun got trapped inside a broken elevator while she was alone at the convent and her sisters were out of town at a convention. Sister Margaret Geary of Notre Dame de Namur in Baltimore was in the elevator for four nights and three days with only a jar of water, some celery sticks and a few cough drops. The electricity went out, so she could not push the doors open, and her cell phone had no signal.

"It was either panic or pray," she later told CNN, viewing the experience as a "gift" and an opportunity to get closer to God. "I believe that God's presence was my strength and my joy—really."[3]

Taking the appropriate spiritual step in the right situation, such as praying when you are in trouble, like Sister Margaret did, or singing praises to God when you are happy is one of the wisest things you can do in life. If you are facing physical or spiritual affliction, remember that there's a season for everything, and this too shall pass. God's healing is right around the corner!

### DOWNLOAD IN PROGRESS

■■■■■■■■■■■■□□□□□□□□□□□□□□□□□□□□□□□□□□□□□□□□□□□□□□□□□□■■■

0%      10%     20%     30%     40%     50%     60%     70%     80%     90%

## Step 2: Call Upon the Cavalry

James 5:14 reads, "Is anyone among you sick? Let them *call the elders of the church* to pray over them and anoint them with oil in the name of the Lord" (emphasis added). In most churches, there is a governing board whose members are sometimes called elders, deacons or bishops because they have acquired wisdom and a certain level of spirituality that sets them apart. In the apostle Paul's letter to Titus, his dear friend and co-laborer in the faith, he unequivocally outlines the types of qualities a man must possess in order to be appointed to the role of an elder:

> He must be blameless, faithful to his wife . . . not overbearing, not quick-tempered, not given to drunkenness, not violent, not pursuing dishonest gain . . . he must be hospitable, one who loves what is good, self-controlled, upright, holy and disciplined . . . [and] encourage others by sound doctrine and refute those who oppose it (Titus 1:6-9).

This long list of requirements gives us the assurance that elders typically are men who are spiritually mature and above reproach in every way. They are what I like to call the "cavalry," a word that describes "the part of a military force composed of troops that serve on horseback," or "armored units of a military force organized for maximum mobility."[4] Like a spine-tingling movie scene with mounted cowboys or soldiers riding onto the battlefield to save the day, you need to look at the elders of your church as lean, mean, fighting machines—men who have spent years being involved in spiritual warfare, lying in the trenches as intercessors for the people in their church. And when you are afflicted, you need to gather these men around you for prayer. It doesn't matter whether it's one elder, two or three, eight or ten; God will work through these spiritual leaders.

Craig Brian Larson, editor of PreachingToday.com, witnessed the remarkable and well-attested power of prayer in the life of a fellow pastor named Kenneth Wallace of central Illinois. He describes Kenneth as "a happy warrior: big voice, thick build, square-jawed, always with a toothy smile." But one day in November, some discomfort in the area of his prostate sent him in to see his physician. Thinking he was going to receive a prescription for what he assumed was an infection, the doctor instead gave him some bad news: a large, malignant tumor had formed on his prostate gland. In fact, it was so large that it had probably been there for more than 10 years. On a scale of 1 to 4 with 4 being the worst, he was a 4.

A specialist in Springfield, Illinois, and doctors at Johns Hopkins University determined that chemotherapy would be useless, surgery too dangerous, and that radiation would cause too many other problems. The cancer was terminal, and they could only give Kenneth medication for pain. Soon, his weight dropped from 217 to 138. Kenneth decided to attend one last statewide meeting of pastors, and in that meeting his fellow pastors gathered around him and cried out to heaven on his behalf. As he headed home later that night, he was encouraged by their concern but still suffering from unbearable pain.

Two months later, his brother, who was also a pastor, visited him at his home. Kenneth was so worn down by the pain that he told his wife and his brother, "Ask God to either heal me or take me." They prayed, and after a while they left. As Kenneth was lying on the couch, he suddenly became aware of a physical sensation he described as "a soothing warm feeling going throughout my body. Every bit of pain and discomfort left."

He tried to sit up but was still very weak. Calling out to his wife, Ann, he said, "Jesus just healed me!" He didn't take his usual pain medication or sleeping pill that night before going to bed, yet for the first time in six months he fell asleep immediately and slept all night. At his next doctor's appointment a week later, Kenneth's doctor was shocked when he saw him, and ordered some tests. The tests were sent to Johns Hopkins University, and the results came back completely negative. Kenneth Wallace was perfectly healed. He lived 12 more years, pastoring his church for a total of 40 years.[5]

Whether God worked through the passionate prayers of godly men at that statewide conference or the prayers of his brother and wife, Kenneth was miraculously restored. His story—and the many others too numerous to detail here—are a powerful reminder that God indeed hears the prayers of His people. And from James's instructions in James 5:14, it seems that when we are in need of healing from physical and spiritual affliction, it's imperative that we receive prayer from the spiritual leaders of our church.

You don't have to call upon an elder specifically; if your church does not have elders or a board of directors, you can go to anyone in the body of believers—a teacher, pastor, youth worker or any godly man or woman who is gifted at praying. I have both witnessed and learned of many miraculous instances when people were healed because Christians gathered around that person and prayed for him or her. So, if you are facing sickness of any kind, call upon the cavalry of prayer warriors and take an important step in God's app to heal your affliction.

**DOWNLOAD IN PROGRESS**

0%      10%      20%      30%      40%      50%      60%      70%      80%      90%

## Step 3: Use a Thimble of an Important Symbol

In his book *God Still Heals,* Dr. Jim Garlow shares about receiving an unusual request when he first became the pastor of a small church in Trenton, New Jersey:

> One Sunday, a lady named Mrs. Bailey came to me and said, "Pastor, I'm sick, and I need you to pray for me."
>
> I froze. I knew virtually nothing about praying and healing, and the blank look on my face must have said so because Mrs. Bailey continued, "The Bible does say to come to elders and ask for prayer, doesn't it?"
>
> For the life of me, I could not remember where that passage was located, but I said, "Yes, it does."
>
> "Well," she said, "You're an elder, and I'm coming to be anointed with oil."
>
> Believe me, at twenty-eight years of age, I certainly didn't feel like an elder. On top of that, I don't recall that I had ever seen someone anointed with oil before that time. I had grown up in a wonderful Christian home and had attended a great church, but we didn't pray for the sick very much at all. By this time I held three master's degrees . . . and I was completing my doctoral studies in

church history, but I still had no idea what she meant when she asked to be anointed with oil. It sounds hilarious now, but all I could think of was a can of motor oil! I needed to stall for time, so I asked Mrs. Bailey to meet me in another part of the church a bit later.

Meanwhile, I went to find a godly woman named Irma Weaver. Irma was about seventy-three years old and had previously served as pastor of this congregation for about ten years. I found her sitting in the sanctuary and raced over to her. "Mrs. Weaver," I said, "we're going to need you downstairs, please. We'd like to anoint Mrs. Bailey with oil." She seemed to know exactly what I was talking about, so I just kept going. "Mrs. Weaver, out of deference to you, I'd like for you to be the one to anoint Mrs. Bailey." To my great relief, she said she would.

As we walked downstairs, I wondered what this was going to look like. Would she pour oil all over Mrs. Bailey? Would she use a whole quart? Would we need to tarp the floor? What actually happened was that Mrs. Weaver took a small vial of clear oil, dabbed a drop onto her finger, and placed it on Mrs. Bailey's forehead. Then she prayed for her. That was all. Looking back, I recall that as a wonderful, spiritual moment. But at the time, I admit, it seemed a little spooky.[6]

In chapter 3, we discussed the multitude of modern uses for oil as we downloaded God's app to break down the walls that divide. Returning to that important theme and staying with James 5:14, we read, "Is anyone among you sick? Let them call the elders of the church to pray over them and *anoint them with oil* in the name of the Lord" (emphasis added). James is saying that the elders should not only pray for the afflicted but also anoint him or her with oil.

Anointing the sick with oil was not a new practice that James was advocating; it was instituted by the Lord. "The oil in Scripture is often a type of Holy Spirit. It is by His power that miracles

occur. It was to be done in Jesus' name, that is, by His authority . . .
The Twelve 'anointed many sick people with oil'" (Mark 6:13).[7]

Gary Holloway's commentary on the book of James explains
it this way:

> Some say oil here is medicinal (cf. Isaiah 1:6; Luke 10:34).
> James is saying, "Take your medicine and pray, too." [Ad-
> ditionally] oil symbolically stood for the special favor and
> blessing of God. Prophets (Isaiah 61:1), priests (Exodus
> 29:7), and kings (1 Samuel 10:1) were all anointed with oil
> to show that God was with them. In this verse, oil symbol-
> izes the blessing of healing from God. The oil does not
> heal; the Lord who hears prayer does (v. 15).
>
> However, one should not be too quick to dismiss the
> power of that symbol. In the Lord's Supper, the bread and
> the fruit of the vine are symbolic of Christ's body and blood.
> In baptism, burial in the water is symbolic of dying and ris-
> ing with Christ. Although these are symbols, they are not
> *mere* symbols that can be dispensed with. In the same way,
> the practice of anointing with oil as a symbol of the power
> of prayer perhaps should be revived in the church.[8]

If you are in need of healing, turn to the elders, spiritual leaders and prayer warriors of your church and request that they use a
thimble of this powerful symbol. As Mrs. Bailey and Mrs. Weaver
of Jim Garlow's church understood, it is the third crucial step in
God's app to heal the afflicted.

**DOWNLOAD IN PROGRESS**

0%    10%    20%    30%    40%    50%    60%    70%    80%    90%

## Step 4: Turn to the One Who Can Turn the Key

Before we move on to the rest of James 5, there is a third and final
takeaway from verse 14, and it is that the elders should pray over
and anoint the sick with oil "in the name of the Lord." No one

would ever do anything in the name of Dudley or Donovan or Sam, but there is something very unique about the name of Jesus. When you study the Bible, you find that the phrase "in the name of the Lord" occurs 28 times in the *New International Version* of the Old Testament; and "in the name of Jesus" occurs 8 times in the New Testament. Whenever you see either phrase, something powerful has happened or is about to happen.

Preaching, baptizing, casting out demons and healing were all done in the name of the Lord or in the name of Jesus. Why? There is *power* in His wonderful name! God has given Jesus authority above all others, and this includes the authority to heal others. Perhaps you've heard Christ referred to as the Great Physician. This term comes from the words Jesus spoke in Luke 5:31-32 after the Pharisees asked Him why He ate with tax collectors and sinners at Matthew's house: "It is not the healthy who need a doctor, but the sick. I have not come to call the righteous, but sinners to repentance."

In Matthew 8, He demonstrates His authority to heal as He completely restores a man with leprosy (see v. 3), a paralytic (see v. 13), a feverish woman (see v. 15), and many who were demon-possessed or had other illnesses (see v. 16). Jesus' authority over death itself becomes astonishingly evident as He brings a little girl back to life in Matthew 9:23-25 and raises Lazarus from the dead in John 11:42-44. What's more, He Himself conquered the grave when He rose from the dead on the third day after His crucifixion (see Matt. 28:1-7; Acts 2:23-24; Col. 2:15) and declared to His disciples before His ascension, "All authority in heaven and on earth has been given to me . . . And surely I am with you always, to the very end of the age" (Matt. 28:18,20). Christ Jesus alone holds the key to healing and to life itself.

Just a few weeks ago, I was asked to speak at the Los Angeles County Jail, which is the largest jail in the world and houses 20,000 inmates.[9] I went with a few other pastors from our church, and we were in a room with about 180 prisoners in blue jumpsuits. I can't say I was nervous, but as a straight-laced boy from the Midwest, I was definitely out of my element, if you know what I mean.

Besides getting to talk to prisoners about the hope that is found in Jesus Christ, the thing that struck me the most about this incredible experience was actually getting *inside* the jail. As we arrived, there were two barbed-wire fences that seemed about as tall as a Sequoia tree and as expansive as Lake Superior. If you were an escapee and happened to get past the first fence without being caught by the guards or by the sniper in the high tower above, you still had to make it up and over the second fence, which was about six feet away. Once you were within that precarious predicament, you would know that escape was not possible.

After we entered through the two fences, a guard met us and gave us our badges. He carried with him a key like I had never seen before. It wasn't your average household key that could snap in a rusty door lock; this was a big, heavy-duty, prison key. The guard took us through the first door, and after we all walked through it, he turned and locked the door behind us. Then he took us through another door and locked that door behind us, and we kept doing this until we had gone through six or seven of these doors. The more doors we went through that were locked behind us, the more nervous I got. At one point, I was so far in that I thought, *Man, I might not ever get out of here!*

So I sort of joked with the guard and said, "Hey, is there any way I can get a copy of that key?"

He looked at me stone-faced, and it was obvious that he was not amused. But as we went through these maximum security doors, I had a thought: *What if you were a prisoner inside that jail and you were behind six, seven, eight locked gates, and a guy comes in and says to you, "You've been pardoned; you're free to go. Here's the key." And he sets the key on the desk and leaves.*

Can you imagine saying, "You know, I don't believe that's the real key; I don't think that thing works. I think this is a trick; it's fake, it's phony, it's not real," and you remain in the state you're in because you don't believe the key is real? In the same way, all of us in one way or another are imprisoned by some kind of affliction—and it's usually sin. As Romans 3:23 says, we've all fallen short of the glory of God; every one of us has gone astray.

However, God comes along through Jesus Christ, and says, "You're forgiven. You're free, and Jesus Christ is the key." When you and I put our faith in Him, when we pray sincerely *in the name of the Lord* for healing from our physical and spiritual affliction, we are turning to the *only* One who has the key. James himself gives us this guarantee: "And the prayer offered in faith will make the sick person well; the Lord will raise them up. If they have sinned, they will be forgiven" (5:15). Dear friend, turn to the only One who has the authority to heal you and set you free.

**DOWNLOAD IN PROGRESS**

0%   10%   20%   30%   40%   50%   60%   70%   80%   90%

## Step 5: Unclog the Drain

When we downloaded God's app to restore a broken heart in chapter 6, we learned that a crucial step in healing our relationships with one another is to *confess our sins to God.* On the flip side, it's interesting to note that in order to heal our spiritual affliction—our relationship with God—we must confess our sins *to each other.* Notice what James 5:16 says: "Confess your sins to each other and pray for each other so that you may be healed."

Whenever I think of sin inside a person's life, I always think of a drain getting clogged. Have you ever had to take on the not-so-fun task of unclogging your bathroom sink? If so, you know first-hand that it's not a job for anyone with a weak stomach. After you remove the drain stopper, you fish around the pipe with a wire hanger or some other makeshift tool until you latch onto something. You tug and tug and pull out something that looks like demon spawn from a horror flick! It's all gray and gooey and hairy and wet. (Hair on your head is awesome, but why does it become so incredibly gross when it's in the sink? I will never understand that uncanny phenomenon.) Quickly, you fling the thing into the trashcan and you vigorously scrub your hands with soap and water while getting over your heebie-jeebies. Suddenly, the water begins to flow freely down the drain without any problem at all. Victory!

Like the grime and gunk that clogs a drain and keeps the water from flowing, the sin and junk in our lives hinder God's Spirit and become a major blockage against Him healing our affliction. Sin is disobedience to God; it's saying, "God, I don't need You or want You." We are then quick to ask the Lord to help us when we get into trouble as a result of this sin. But Psalm 66:18 makes this poignant assertion: "If I had cherished sin in my heart, the Lord would not have listened"; therefore, we must remove the junk in our lives that prevents His Spirit from flowing freely through us.

James divulges in verse 16 that one critical way we can unclog the drain and clean out our sin is by confessing our sins to one another. If you've stolen from someone, slandered, judged or been jealous of that person, go to that person in love and humility, confess your sins and ask for forgiveness. Additionally, if you have been concealing a certain sin in your life, go to a believer whom you trust, confess that sin and cover each other in ardent prayer, as James instructs.

We know from the Scriptures that God desires a sense of community among His children and that there is power when we, as believers, come together. Just look at what Jesus said in Matthew 18:20: "For where two or three are gathered together in My name, I am there in the midst of them" (*NKJV*). Supernatural strength is unlocked when God's community is gathered together; and as we deal with sin as a community, we help to maintain spiritual purity in the Church.

If you were a sheep that wandered away from the flock to nurse your wounds, you'd become susceptible to all kinds of dangers. There's the scorching heat of the day, cold nights, wolves and other predators, brambles in which to get caught and pits in which to fall. You would be ripe for the picking because of any one of these risks. Therefore, when you are seeking healing from physical or spiritual affliction, remain with the Shepherd—the Lord Jesus Christ—and you along with the rest of the flock will find protection from those who wish to harm you or lead you astray.

James continues, in the rest of verse 16: "The prayer of a righteous person is powerful and effective." But what is a righteous person? To be righteous is to be in "right standing" with God. It means that you walk before Him faithfully, with wholehearted devotion and do what is good in His eyes, just like King Hezekiah, whom we learned about earlier in our download. Righteousness is obeying God's Word and holding fast to integrity, purity, honesty, goodness and love. And once we become in "right standing" with God through confession and prayer, what results is that our prayers become powerful and effective because the Holy Spirit is enabled to flow freely once again!

## Step 6: Press Redial

It was a spiritual showdown like no other. The prophet Elijah announced to Ahab, the King of Israel, that there was going to be a great drought in the land because the people had abandoned God's commands and followed idols (see 1 Kings 17:1; 18:18). Three years later, and still no rain, Elijah instructed King Ahab to meet him on top of Mount Carmel, along with the people of Israel and the 450 prophets of the false god Baal.

Elijah faced the king and the crowd and said, "How long will you waver between two opinions? If the LORD is God, follow him; but if Baal is God, follow him" (1 Kings 18:21). Then he challenged the 450 prophets to a duel, saying, in essence, "You go build an altar to Baal over there and I will build an altar to the one and only God over here. We'll put a bull on each altar. You call on your god and I'll call on mine, and the god who answers by fire—he is God!"

So the prophets agreed, and they prepared their altar. They made total fools of themselves as they danced around their altar, cut themselves, hollered and wailed to a god who didn't exist. And there was no answer. Then, Elijah doused his altar with water three times so there wouldn't be any doubt. He prayed solemnly, asking God to let it be known that very moment that He is God, and that He is turning the people's hearts back to Him.

As soon as Elijah finished his simple prayer, the fire of the Lord fell from the sky and burned up the sacrifice, the wood, the stones and the soil, and licked up all the water that had been poured on the altar. When the people saw this, they fell on their faces and cried, "The LORD—he is God! The LORD—he is God!" (v. 39). A spiritual cleansing ensued, as Elijah had the 450 prophets of Baal killed.

Following the victory, Elijah tackled the drought issue by praying for rain (see 1 Kings 18:16-45). Take a look at what James 5:17-18 says: "Elijah was a human being, even as we are. He prayed earnestly that it would not rain, and it did not rain on the land for three and a half years. Again he prayed, and the heavens gave rain, and the earth produced its crops."

If we return to 1 Kings 18:43-44, we see that, in fact, Elijah prayed *seven times* on top of Mount Carmel for it to rain, until a small cloud formed over the sea. Then the sky turned black with clouds, the winds blew and a heavy rain began to fall (see v. 45). James asserts that Elijah was an ordinary person like you and me, and yet his persistent and faithful prayer caused the heavens to open and revive the land from a terrible, three-year drought. When we pray, we must follow Elijah's example; we mustn't give up, but continue to ask God in faith to come and rescue us from the droughts of life.

One afternoon, when one of my daughters was very young, I placed her in her crib for naptime. I went downstairs and had just sat down in my chair when I heard her little voice calling for me. She called my name not once or twice, but over and over and over again. Now, I know this totally defies "Parenting 101," but I was fascinated by her determination and thought to myself, *If she calls my name 100 times, I am going to run right back in there for her.* Sitting on the edge of my seat in utter amazement, I counted 96, 97, 98, 99 . . . The second I heard "Daddy" that one hundredth time, I ran upstairs and scooped my little girl from her crib and held her in my arms.

Thankfully, our Father in heaven is not going to sit on His throne and count how many times we call for deliverance. However, this story illustrates the patience and perseverance we should demonstrate as we call upon the Lord during times of affliction. Like the parable of the persistent widow in Luke 18, which Jesus told His disciples "to show them that they should always pray and not give up" (v. 1), my daughter wouldn't have called for her daddy 100 times had she not truly believed in her heart that I would eventually come for her. How much more is our Abba Father faithful to come for us? He's on His way. Keep calling.

**DOWNLOAD COMPLETE!**

0%    10%    20%    30%    40%    50%    60%    70%    80%    90%

When Jesus returned to the town of Capernaum, His reputation as an authoritative teacher and healer caused the people to gather around Him in large numbers. Four men went to great lengths to get through the crowd and brought to Jesus a paralyzed man who was lying on a mat. When Jesus saw their faith, He said to the paralyzed man, "Son, your sins are forgiven" (Mark 2:5). However, some teachers of law were sitting there and thought to themselves, *This man is blaspheming! Who can forgive sins but God alone?*

Knowing their thoughts, Jesus answered, "Which is easier: to say to this paralyzed man, 'Your sins are forgiven,' or to say, 'Get up, take your mat and walk'? But I want you to know that the Son of Man has authority on earth to forgive sins.' So he said to the man, 'I tell you, get up, take your mat and go home.' He got up, took his mat and walked out in full view of them all. This amazed everyone and they praised God, saying, 'We have never seen anything like this!'" (Mark 2:9-12).

This story epitomizes Jesus Christ's authority to heal us both physically and spiritually; the two go hand in hand. As believers, we have a resource that no doctor, medication or healthcare plan can rival. We have access to the Lord God Almighty, who made us and has the infinite power to give and restore life. By downloading God's app to heal your affliction, here is what you do when you need healing:

- Acknowledge that there is a season for everything and do what is appropriate in each season; if you are in trouble, pray, and if you are happy, sing songs of praise.
- Call upon the cavalry, the elders and spiritual leaders of your church to pray for you.
- Use a thimble of an important symbol—oil—which represents God's Spirit and blessing.
- Turn to the only One who can turn the key, Jesus; God has given Him all authority to heal you and set you free.
- Unclog the drain by confessing your sins to one another and praying for one another.
- Press redial—keep calling on God through faithful prayer; don't give up!

My young friend Hailey sits in the front row at church every Sunday. She once shared with me that Job is her favorite book of the Bible because—though he was terribly afflicted and lost everything that was dear to him—this great man of faith never doubted God. Despite seemingly endless surgeries, doctors' visits and a negative prognosis, Hailey says with unshakable resolve, "I keep believing, and I have faith. The Holy Spirit is living inside me, watching over me. I pray every night and He helps me get through everything." (To see my interview with Hailey, please visit the "Videos" section of www.GodHasAnApp.com.)

What an inspiration she is to others to persevere with a steadfast hope, no matter how they may be afflicted! We serve a God who hears our prayers. As Psalm 9:18 declares, "But God will never forget the needy; the hope of the afflicted will never perish," Thank You, Lord, for caring for the afflicted and meeting our every need.

# Conclusion

Congratulations! By completing this book, you have successfully downloaded eight extraordinary apps from God to turn your stress into joy, help you overcome temptation, break down the walls that divide, resuscitate a dying faith, curb your profanity, restore a broken heart and heal your affliction. My prayer is that through this spiritual journey, you have been enriched and refreshed and that you are fully convinced that God indeed has an app for your every need!

Yes, our heavenly Father has an answer for anything you are struggling with or in search of. And His solutions really are not that difficult to find if one simply searches within the one Book that has sold more copies than any book ever written in the history of the world—the Bible.

In the same way that we must have physical nourishment to live from day to day, we must also have spiritual nourishment to feed our inner man. God, our Creator, did not just leave us to blindly survive on our own; He provided a blueprint, a lamp to direct our footsteps. The Bible is the instruction manual that enables us to get the most out of life. It contains answers for every problem we face, and it is my sincere hope that, through the course of this essential download, you were led to pick up a copy of God's Word and begin to read it on your own.

I once heard a story about a Native American man who had two dogs that fought all the time. When asked which dog usually won the fight, the man replied, "The one I feed the most." Most of us have an inner struggle between the flesh and the spirit, each vying for our commitment to follow God or *not* to follow God. It's like a tug-of-war going on within us between good and evil. Which one is going to win? Whichever one we feed the most. In order for you to have total victory in this life, you need to be constantly feeding the spirit, the good man, within you.

I have always held the position that God has an answer or an app for any question you are pondering or decision you are facing. He really does. You name the issue—greed, provision, lust, wisdom, addiction, relationships, love, raising children, learning how to forgive or facing temptation of any kind. Even if there is something that is *not* mentioned in the Bible (such as "Where should I live?" or "What kind of car should I drive?"), God has advice and wisdom for you. He enables you to define what is important in life and He leads you to walk in the center of His will as you obey and follow His commandments.

If you read the Bible every day, looking for God's apps within the Scriptures, you will develop a spiritual mindset and you will actually begin to adopt the mind of Christ. You will be able to make the right decisions based on the Word of God and the leading of the Spirit of God that is inside of you. Whatever you're facing and whatever you're dealing with, I want to challenge you to find a Bible reading plan and begin to carve time out of your busy schedule to allow God to teach you His will and give you direction for your life.

Included in the back of this book is a Bible reading guide. All it takes is a few chapters a day to get through the entire Bible in one year. Once you accomplish this task, you will feel blessed and nurtured beyond measure. If you don't own a Bible, you can purchase one to carry around with you or upload the Bible in a Year app onto your smartphone or computer. I have produced 52 videos—one per week—that will introduce what you are about to read as we go through the Bible together. Visit www.GodHasAn App.com for more information.

Psalm 1:3 tells us that the person who delights in the law of the Lord and who meditates on it day and night will be like "a tree that is planted by streams of water, which yields its fruit in season and whose leaf does not wither—whatever they do prospers." Then, Psalm 119 is filled with all the blessings and benefits one will enjoy when he or she searches and follows God's instructions.

My encouragement to you is that if you have tried everything else to find satisfaction in life, why not try seeking God? Apply a sincere effort to read God's Word and to find His will for your life. More than anything this life has to offer, the Word of God is eternal because God Himself is eternal. Just look at what Psalm 112:1-9 so brilliantly proclaims:

Blessed are those who fear the LORD, who find great delight in his commands.
Their children will be mighty in the land;
  the generation of the upright will be blessed.
Wealth and riches are in their houses,
  and their righteousness endures forever.
Even in darkness light dawns for the upright,
  for those who are gracious and compassionate and
  righteous.
Good will come to those who are generous and lend freely,
  who conduct their affairs with justice.
Surely the righteous will never be shaken;
  they will be remembered forever.
They will have no fear of bad news;
  their hearts are steadfast, trusting in the LORD.
Their hearts are secure, they will have no fear;
  in the end they will look in triumph on their foes.
They have freely scattered their gifts to the poor,
  their righteousness endures forever;
  their horn will be lifted high in honor.

May God give you the ability to see the worth and value of God's precious Word. In it you will find life, love, peace, rest, joy, salvation, blessings and answers. God has an app for whatever you need help with, so enjoy the journey and fall in love with the One who is known as the Truth of the Ages.

# God Has an App to
# Help You Find Encouragement in the Bible

No matter what your external circumstances may be, your security in life rests on the internal peace you discover when you put your faith and hope in God's promises. Listed below are just a few of the biblical promises that will give you confidence when you are facing some of life's most common trials.

Anger . . . . . . . . . . . . . . . . . Romans 12:17-21
Anxiety . . . . . . . . . . . . . . . Philippians 4:6-7; 1 Peter 5:6-11
Apathy . . . . . . . . . . . . . . . . James 5:17
Bitterness . . . . . . . . . . . . . 1 Corinthians 13:4-7
Brokenhearted . . . . . . . . Psalm 34:18
Confusion . . . . . . . . . . . . 1 Corinthians 14:33
Criticism . . . . . . . . . . . . . . Psalm 27
Defeat . . . . . . . . . . . . . . . . 2 Corinthians 4:8
Delay . . . . . . . . . . . . . . . . . 2 Corinthians 4:8
Depression . . . . . . . . . . . . Psalm 119:139-144
Disappointment . . . . . . . Romans 8:28; Psalm 139:16
Doubt . . . . . . . . . . . . . . . . Matthew 17:20
Failure . . . . . . . . . . . . . . . Proverbs 24:16
Fear . . . . . . . . . . . . . . . . . . Isaiah 41:10; 2 Timothy 1:7
Forgiveness . . . . . . . . . . . Romans 8:1; 1 John 1:9; James 5:15
Grief . . . . . . . . . . . . . . . . . Psalm 23:4
Health . . . . . . . . . . . . . . . . 1 Corinthians 6:19-20
Hunger . . . . . . . . . . . . . . . Matthew 4:4
Hurry . . . . . . . . . . . . . . . . Lamentations 3:25-26
Impatience . . . . . . . . . . . . Psalm 27:14

Impossibilities .......... Luke 18:27
Inability ............... 2 Corinthians 9:8
Inadequacy ............. Romans 11:33-36; Philippians 4:13
Lacking Direction ...... Proverbs 3:5-6
Lacking Intelligence .... James 1:5
Lacking Wisdom ....... 1 Corinthians 1:30
Loneliness ............... Deuteronomy 31:6; Hebrews 13:5-8
Mourning ............... Matthew 5:4
Poverty ................. Philippians 4:19
Pressure ................ Philippians 4:13
Pride .................. James 4:10
Rejection ............... Romans 8:39
Sorrow ................. Jeremiah 31:13
Stress .................. Philippians 4:6-8
Temptation ............ 1 Corinthians 10:13
Tiredness .............. Isaiah 40:31
Uncertainty ............ Philippians 3:12-14
Unforgiveness .......... Matthew 18:21-22, Luke 17:3-5
Unloved ............... 1 John 3:1
Values ................. 1 John 2:15-17
Weakness .............. 2 Corinthians 12:9
Weariness ............. Matthew 11:28-30
Worry ................. Matthew 6:31-34; 1 Peter 5:7

## God Has an App to
# Take You Through the Bible in One Year

The following guide will help you to easily read through the Bible in one year. Read the passage of Scripture listed for each day, check the boxes as you go, and be encouraged by your progress. If you miss a day or two, don't give up! You will be proud of yourself at the end of one year, and your spirit will be enriched by all that you have learned from God's Word. You may also download the "Bible in a Year" app by searching "Bible in a Year" in your smartphone's app marketplace—look for the dark blue icon that has a red bor-
 der and the words "READ BIBLE" inside. You can also visit www.GodHasAnApp.com for more information and to see a cool video about how the app works.

❏ Day 1: Genesis 1–4

❏ Day 2: Genesis 5–8

❏ Day 3: Genesis 9–12

❏ Day 4: Genesis 13–17

❏ Day 5: Genesis 18–20

❏ Day 6: Genesis 21–23

❏ Day 7: Genesis 24–25

❏ Day 8: Genesis 26–28

❏ Day 9: Genesis 29–31

❏ Day 10: Genesis 32–35

❏ Day 11: Genesis 36–38

❏ Day 12: Genesis 39–41

❏ Day 13: Genesis 42–43

❏ Day 14: Genesis 44–46

❏ Day 15: Genesis 47–50

❏ Day 16: Exodus 1–4

❏ Day 17: Exodus 5–7

❏ Day 18: Exodus 8–10

❏ Day 19: Exodus 11–13

❏ Day 20: Exodus 14–16

❏ Day 21: Exodus 17–20

❏ Day 22: Exodus 21–23

❏ Day 23: Exodus 24–27

❏ Day 24: Exodus 28–30

❏ Day 25: Exodus 31–34

❏ Day 26: Exodus 35–37

❏ Day 27: Exodus 38–40

❏ Day 28: Matthew 1–4

❑ Day 29: Matthew 5–6

❑ Day 30: Matthew 7–9

❑ Day 31: Matthew 10–11

❑ Day 32: Matthew 12–13

❑ Day 33: Matthew 14–17

❑ Day 34: Matthew 18–20

❑ Day 35: Matthew 21–22

❑ Day 36: Matthew 23–24

❑ Day 37: Matthew 25–26

❑ Day 38: Matthew 27–28

❑ Day 39: Leviticus 1–4

❑ Day 40: Leviticus 5–7

❑ Day 41: Leviticus 8–10

❑ Day 42: Leviticus 11–13

❑ Day 43: Leviticus 14–15

❑ Day 44: Leviticus 16–18

❑ Day 45: Leviticus 19–21

❑ Day 46: Leviticus 22–23

❑ Day 47: Leviticus 24–25

❑ Day 48: Leviticus 26–27

❑ Day 49: Mark 1–3

❑ Day 50: Mark 4–5

❑ Day 51: Mark 6–7

❑ Day 52: Mark 8–9

❑ Day 53: Mark 10–11

❑ Day 54: Mark 12–13

❑ Day 55: Mark 14

❑ Day 56: Mark 15–16

❑ Day 57: Numbers 1–2

❑ Day 58: Numbers 3–4

❑ Day 59: Numbers 5–6

❑ Day 60: Numbers 7

❑ Day 61: Numbers 8–10

❑ Day 62: Numbers 11–13

❑ Day 63: Numbers 14–15

❑ Day 64: Numbers 16–18

❑ Day 65: Numbers 19–21

❑ Day 66: Numbers 22–24

❑ Day 67: Numbers 25–26

❑ Day 68: Numbers 27–29

❑ Day 69: Numbers 30–32

❑ Day 70: Numbers 33–36

❑ Day 71: Luke 1–2

❑ Day 72: Luke 3–4

❑ Day 73: Luke 5–6

❑ Day 74: Luke 7–8

❑ Day 75: Luke 9–10

❑ Day 76: Luke 11–12

❑ Day 77: Luke 13–15

❑ Day 78: Luke 16–18

❑ Day 79: Luke 19–20

❑ Day 80: Luke 21–22

❑ Day 81: Luke 23–24

❑ Day 82: Deuteronomy 1–2

❑ Day 83: Deuteronomy 3–4

❑ Day 84: Deuteronomy 5–8

❑ Day 85: Deuteronomy 9–11

❑ Day 86: Deuteronomy 12–15

❑ Day 87: Deuteronomy 16–19

❑ Day 88: Deuteronomy 20–22

❑ Day 89: Deuteronomy 23–25

❑ Day 90: Deuteronomy 26–27

❑ Day 91: Deuteronomy 28–29

❑ Day 92: Deuteronomy 30–32

❑ Day 93: Deuteronomy 33–34

❑ Day 94: John 1–2

❑ Day 95: John 3–4

❑ Day 96: John 5–6

❑ Day 97: John 7–8

❑ Day 98: John 9–10

❑ Day 99: John 11–12

❑ Day 100: John 13–15

❑ Day 101: John 16–17

❑ Day 102: John 18–19

❑ Day 103: John 20–21

❑ Day 104: Joshua 1–4

❑ Day 105: Joshua 5–7

❑ Day 106: Joshua 8–10

❑ Day 107: Joshua 11–13

❑ Day 108: Joshua 14–17

❑ Day 109: Joshua 18–20

❑ Day 110: Joshua 21–22

❑ Day 111: Joshua 23–24

❑ Day 112: Acts 1–3

❑ Day 113: Acts 4–5

❑ Day 114: Acts 6–7

❑ Day 115: Acts 8–9

❑ Day 116: Acts 10–11

❑ Day 117: Acts 12–13

❑ Day 118: Acts 14–15

❑ Day 119: Acts 16–17

❑ Day 120: Acts 18–19

❑ Day 121: Acts 20–21

❑ Day 122: Acts 22–23

❑ Day 123: Acts 24–26

❑ Day 124: Acts 27–28

❑ Day 125: Judges 1–3

❑ Day 126: Judges 4–5

❑ Day 127: Judges 6–8

❑ Day 128: Judges 9–10

❑ Day 129: Judges 11–13

❑ Day 130: Judges 14–16

❑ Day 131: Judges 17–19

❑ Day 132: Judges 20–21

❑ Day 133: Ruth 1–4

❑ Day 134: Romans 1–3

❑ Day 135: Romans 4–7

❑ Day 136: Romans 8–10

❑ Day 137: Romans 11–14

❑ Day 138: Romans 15–16

❑ Day 139: 1 Samuel 1–3

❑ Day 140: 1 Samuel 4–7

❑ Day 141: 1 Samuel 8–12

❑ Day 142: 1 Samuel 13–14

❑ Day 143: 1 Samuel 15–16

❑ Day 144: 1 Samuel 17–18

❑ Day 145: 1 Samuel 19–21

❑ Day 146: 1 Samuel 22–24

❑ Day 147: 1 Samuel 25–27

❑ Day 148: 1 Samuel 28–31

❑ Day 149: 2 Samuel 1–3

❑ Day 150: 2 Samuel 4–7

❑ Day 151: 2 Samuel 8–11

❑ Day 152: 2 Samuel 12–13

❑ Day 153: 2 Samuel 14–16

❑ Day 154: 2 Samuel 17–19

❑ Day 155: 2 Samuel 20–22

❑ Day 156: 2 Samuel 23–24

❑ Day 157: 1 Corinthians 1–4

❑ Day 158: 1 Corinthians 5–9

❑ Day 159: 1 Corinthians 10–13

❑ Day 160: 1 Corinthians 14–16

❑ Day 161: 1 Kings 1–2

❑ Day 162: 1 Kings 3–5

❑ Day 163: 1 Kings 6–7

❑ Day 164: 1 Kings 8–9

❑ Day 165: 1 Kings 10–12

❑ Day 166: 1 Kings 13–15

❑ Day 167: 1 Kings 16–18

❑ Day 168: 1 Kings 19–20

❑ Day 169: 1 Kings 21–22

❑ Day 170: 2 Kings 1–3

❑ Day 171: 2 Kings 4–5

❑ Day 172: 2 Kings 6–8

❑ Day 173: 2 Kings 9–10

❑ Day 174: 2 Kings 11–13

❑ Day 175: 2 Kings 14–16

❑ Day 176: 2 Kings 17–18

❑ Day 177: 2 Kings 19–21

❑ Day 178: 2 Kings 22–23

❑ Day 179: 2 Kings 24–25

❑ Day 180: 2 Corinthians 1–4

❑ Day 181: 2 Corinthians 5–9

❑ Day 182: 2 Corinthians 10–13

❑ Day 183: 1 Chronicles 1–2

❑ Day 184: 1 Chronicles 3–4

❑ Day 185: 1 Chronicles 5–6

❑ Day 186: 1 Chronicles 7–9

❑ Day 187: 1 Chronicles 10–12

❑ Day 188: 1 Chronicles 13–16

❑ Day 189: 1 Chronicles 17–19

❑ Day 190: 1 Chronicles 20–23

❑ Day 191: 1 Chronicles 24–26

❑ Day 192: 1 Chronicles 27–29

❑ Day 193: 2 Chronicles 1–4

❑ Day 194: 2 Chronicles 5–7

❑ Day 195: 2 Chronicles 8–11

❑ Day 196: 2 Chronicles 12–16

❑ Day 197: 2 Chronicles 17–20

❑ Day 198: 2 Chronicles 21–24

❑ Day 199: 2 Chronicles 25–28

❑ Day 200: 2 Chronicles 29–31

❑ Day 201: 2 Chronicles 32–34

❑ Day 202: 2 Chronicles 35–36

❑ Day 203: Galatians 1–3

❑ Day 204: Galatians 4–6

❑ Day 205: Ezra 1–4

❑ Day 206: Ezra 5–7

❑ Day 207: Ezra 8–10

❑ Day 208: Ephesians 1–3

❑ Day 209: Ephesians 4–6

❑ Day 210: Nehemiah 1–3

❑ Day 211: Nehemiah 4–7

❑ Day 212: Nehemiah 8–10

❑ Day 213: Nehemiah 11–13

❑ Day 214: Philippians 1–4

❑ Day 215: Esther 1–5

❑ Day 216: Esther 6–10

❑ Day 217: Colossians 1–4

❑ Day 218: Job 1–4

❑ Day 219: Job 5–8

❑ Day 220: Job 9–12

❑ Day 221: Job 13–16

❑ Day 222: Job 17–20

❑ Day 223: Job 21–24

❑ Day 224: Job 25–30

❑ Day 225: Job 31–34

❑ Day 226: Job 35–38

❑ Day 227: Job 39–42

❑ Day 228: Psalms 1–8

❑ Day 229: Psalms 9–17

❑ Day 230: 1 Thessalonians 1–5

❑ Day 231: Psalms 18–21

❑ Day 232: Psalms 22–27

❑ Day 233: 2 Thessalonians 1–3

❑ Day 234: Psalms 28–33

❑ Day 235: Psalms 34–37

❑ Day 236: Proverbs 1–3

❑ Day 237: Psalms 38–42

❑ Day 238: Proverbs 4–7

❑ Day 239: 1 Timothy 1–6

❑ Day 240: Psalms 43–49

❑ Day 241: Psalms 50–55

❑ Day 242: Proverbs 8–11

❑ Day 243: 2 Timothy 1–4

❑ Day 244: Psalms 56–61

- ❑ Day 245: Psalms 62–68
- ❑ Day 246: Proverbs 12–14
- ❑ Day 247: Psalms 69–72
- ❑ Day 248: Titus and Philemon
- ❑ Day 249: Psalms 73–77
- ❑ Day 250: Psalms 78–80
- ❑ Day 251: Proverbs 15–17
- ❑ Day 252: Psalms 81–88
- ❑ Day 253: Hebrews 1–4
- ❑ Day 254: Hebrews 5–8
- ❑ Day 255: Hebrews 9–10
- ❑ Day 256: Hebrews 11–13
- ❑ Day 257: Psalms 89–94
- ❑ Day 258: Psalms 95–103
- ❑ Day 259: Proverbs 18–20
- ❑ Day 260: James 1–5
- ❑ Day 261: Psalms 104–106
- ❑ Day 262: Psalms 107–111
- ❑ Day 263: Proverbs 21–23
- ❑ Day 264: 1 Peter 1–5
- ❑ Day 265: Psalms 112–118
- ❑ Day 266: Proverbs 24–26
- ❑ Day 267: Ecclesiastes 1–4
- ❑ Day 268: Ecclesiastes 5–8
- ❑ Day 269: Ecclesiastes 9–12
- ❑ Day 270: Psalm 119
- ❑ Day 271: Proverbs 27–29
- ❑ Day 272: Proverbs 30–31
- ❑ Day 273: 2 Peter 1–3
- ❑ Day 274: Song of Solomon 1–4
- ❑ Day 275: Song of Solomon 5–8
- ❑ Day 276: Isaiah 1–3
- ❑ Day 277: Isaiah 4–8
- ❑ Day 278: Isaiah 9–11
- ❑ Day 279: Isaiah 12–14
- ❑ Day 280: Isaiah 15–19
- ❑ Day 281: Isaiah 20–24
- ❑ Day 282: Isaiah 25–28
- ❑ Day 283: Isaiah 29–31
- ❑ Day 284: Isaiah 32–34
- ❑ Day 285: Isaiah 35–37
- ❑ Day 286: Isaiah 38–40
- ❑ Day 287: Isaiah 41–43
- ❑ Day 288: Isaiah 44–46
- ❑ Day 289: Isaiah 47–49
- ❑ Day 290: Isaiah 50–52
- ❑ Day 291: Isaiah 53–56
- ❑ Day 292: Isaiah 57–59
- ❑ Day 293: Isaiah 60–63
- ❑ Day 294: Isaiah 64–66
- ❑ Day 295: Psalms 120–133
- ❑ Day 296: 1 John 1–5
- ❑ Day 297: Jeremiah 1–3
- ❑ Day 298: Jeremiah 4–5
- ❑ Day 299: Jeremiah 6–8
- ❑ Day 300: Jeremiah 9–11
- ❑ Day 301: Jeremiah 12–14
- ❑ Day 302: Jeremiah 15–17
- ❑ Day 303: Jeremiah 18–21
- ❑ Day 304: Jeremiah 22–24
- ❑ Day 305: Jeremiah 25–27
- ❑ Day 306: Jeremiah 28–30
- ❑ Day 307: Jeremiah 31–32
- ❑ Day 308: Jeremiah 33–36
- ❑ Day 309: Jeremiah 37–39
- ❑ Day 310: Jeremiah 40–43
- ❑ Day 311: Jeremiah 44–46
- ❑ Day 312: Jeremiah 47–48
- ❑ Day 313: Jeremiah 49
- ❑ Day 314: Jeremiah 50
- ❑ Day 315: Jeremiah 51–52
- ❑ Day 316: Psalms 134–140

❑ Day 317: 2, 3 John and Jude

❑ Day 318: Lamentations 1–2

❑ Day 319: Lamentations 3–5

❑ Day 320: Ezekiel 1–4

❑ Day 321: Ezekiel 5–8

❑ Day 322: Ezekiel 9–12

❑ Day 323: Ezekiel 13–15

❑ Day 324: Ezekiel 16–17

❑ Day 325: Ezekiel 18–20

❑ Day 326: Ezekiel 21–22

❑ Day 327: Ezekiel 23–24

❑ Day 328: Ezekiel 25–27

❑ Day 329: Ezekiel 28–30

❑ Day 330: Ezekiel 31–32

❑ Day 331: Ezekiel 33–35

❑ Day 332: Ezekiel 36–38

❑ Day 333: Ezekiel 39–40

❑ Day 334: Ezekiel 41–43

❑ Day 335: Ezekiel 44–46

❑ Day 336: Ezekiel 47–48

❑ Day 337: Psalms 141–150

❑ Day 338: Daniel 1–3

❑ Day 339: Daniel 4–5

❑ Day 340: Daniel 6–8

❑ Day 341: Daniel 9–12

❑ Day 342: Revelation 1–3

❑ Day 343: Revelation 4–7

❑ Day 344: Revelation 8–11

❑ Day 345: Revelation 12–14

❑ Day 346: Revelation 15–17

❑ Day 347: Revelation 18–19

❑ Day 348: Revelation 20–22

❑ Day 349: Hosea 1–4

❑ Day 350: Hosea 5–9

❑ Day 351: Hosea 10–14

❑ Day 352: Joel 1–3

❑ Day 353: Amos 1–4

❑ Day 354: Amos 5–9

❑ Day 355: Obadiah

❑ Day 356: Jonah

❑ Day 357: Micah 1–4

❑ Day 358: Micah 5–7

❑ Day 359: Nahum 1–3

❑ Day 360: Habakkuk 1–3

❑ Day 361: Zephaniah 1–3

❑ Day 362: Haggai 1–2

❑ Day 363: Zechariah 1–5

❑ Day 364: Zechariah 6-10

❑ Day 365: Zechariah 11-14

# Endnotes

**Introduction: God Has an App for Your Every Need**

1. Apple has 425,000 applications for the iPhone (see http://www.apple.com/ iphone/apps-for-iphone/) and 90,000 apps for the iPad (see http://itech-buzz.com/ 5584/does-anyone-know-how-many-apps-are-in-the-market-for-android/). It is estimated that Android has more than 100,000 apps (see http://www. android guys.com/ 2010/07/10/android-market-hit-100000-apps-month/) and that BlackBerry has more than 10,000 (see http://www.zdnet.com /blog/mobile-gadgeteer/blackberry-appworld-passes-10000-apps/3856).

2. Jonny Evans, "Apple's 12 Billion Reasons," *ComputerWorld*, July 19, 2011. http://blogs.computerworld.com/18648/apples_12_billion_reasons.

3. Eric Brantner, "Nine Weirdest iPhone Apps," Directory Journal, January 12, 2010. http://www.dirjournal.com/entertainment-journal/9-weirdest-iphone-apps/.

4. "Angry Birds," Wikipedia.com. http://en.wikipedia.org/wiki/Angry_Birds.

5. "Depression Statistics," Depression Treatment, Signs, Medication, Causes, Test at Clinical Depression Center, 2010 data. http://depressiontreatment help.org/depression-statistics.php.

6. "Key Findings," American Psychological Association, 2010. http://www.apa.org/ news/press/releases/stress/key-findings.aspx.

7. "Summary of Health Statistics for U.S. Adults: National Health Interview Survey," Centers for Disease Control and Prevention, series 10, no. 249, December 2010. http://www.cdc.gov/nchs/data/series/sr_10/sr10_249.pdf

8. "Divorce Statistics," statistics from Jennifer Baker, Forest Institute of Professional Psychology, Springfield. http://www.divorcestatistics.org/.

9. "Virtual World," Wikipedia.org. http://en.wikipedia.org/wiki/Virtual_world.

10. "Suicide in the U.S.: Statistics and Prevention," National Institute of Mental Health, No. 06-4594. http://www.nimh.nih.gov/health/publications/sui cide-in-the-us-statistics-and-prevention/index.shtml.

11. "Russell Conwell," Wikipedia.org. http://en.wikipedia.org/wiki/Russell_Conwell.

12. "Acres of Diamonds," Temple University, 2011. http://www.temple.edu/ about/Acres_of_Diamonds.htm.

13. From reading Acts 21:18 and Galatians 1:19, 2:12, we can conclude that James is the head of the Jerusalem Church.

14. "World Population to Hit 7 Billion this Month," CTV News, October 1, 2011. http://m.ctv.ca/topstories/20111016/world-population-to-hit-seven-billion-111016.html.

15. "Application," Dictionary.com. http://dictionary.reference.com/browse/ap plication?fromRef=true&rh=dictionary.reference.com&__utma=1.15461 19474.1284397204.1286901769.1301008099.15&__utmb=1.1.10.130100

8099&__utmc=1&__utmx=-&__utmz=1.1286392191.6.3.utmcsr=dictionary. reference.com|utmccn=(referral)|utmcmd=referral|utmcct=/&__utmv=- &__utmk= 50917673.

16. "Application Software," Wikipedia.org. http://en.wikipedia.org/wiki/Appli cation_software.

**Chapter 1: God Has an App to Turn Stress into Joy**

1. "James 1," *IVP New Testament Commentaries.* http://www.biblegateway.com/ resources/commentaries/IVP-NT/Jas/Jamess-Greeting.
2. "Introduction to James," *ESV Study Bible.* http://www.esvstudybible.org/ sb/objects/introduction-to-james.html
3. Benjamin Franklin, from a letter to Jean-Baptiste Leroy, 1789, cited in *The Works of Benjamin Franklin,* 1817. http://www.phrases.org.uk/meanings/ death-and-taxes.html.
4. "Trial," Dictonary.com. http://dictionary.reference.com/browse/trial.
5. "Stress," Dictonary.com. http://dictionary.reference.com/browse/stress.
6. "Stress in America Findings," American Psychological Association, No- vember 9, 2010. http://www.apa.org/news/press/releases/stress/national- report.pdf.
7. Elex Michaelson, "Study Shows Angelenos Most Stressed in Nation," KABC- TV Los Angeles, California, November 10, 2010. http://abclocal.go.com/ kabc/story?section=news/local/los_angeles&id=7775744.
8. "Key Findings," American Psychological Association, 2011. http://www.apa.org/ news/press/releases/stress/key-findings.aspx.
9. Will Rogers, quoted in the *New York Times,* April 29, 1930. http://www.quo tationspage.com/quote/136.html.
10. Michael Bronson, "How Many People Die on an Average Day?" Bible Help.org. http://www.biblehelp.org/dieday.htm.
11. "Persecution: Some Uncomfortable Facts," SeekingTruth, 2010. http://www.seek ingtruth.co.uk/persecution.htm.
12. "James 1," *IVP New Testament Commentaries.* http://www.biblegateway.com/ resources/commentaries/IVP-NT/Jas/Trials-574.
13. "Glenn Cunningham," Wikipedia.org. http://en.wikipedia.org/wiki/Glenn_ Cunningham_(athlete).
14. Harry Emerson Fosdick, *On Being a Real Person* (New York, HarperCollins, 1943).

**Chapter 2: God Has an App to Overcome Temptation**

1. Carl's Jr. is called Hardee's for those of you in the eastern half of the United States.
2. The word is *anthropinos.* You can read about it in Spiros Zodhiates, ed., *The Complete Word Study Dictionary: New Testament* (Chattanooga, TN: AMG Pub- lishers, 1993).

3. Wayne E. Oates, *Temptation: A Biblical and Psychological Approach* (Louisville, KY: Westminster/John Knox Press, 1991), p. 22.

4. Here's a modern version I enjoy from *The Emperor's New Groove*: http://www.you tube.com/watch?v=Fv-sKP17xTw.

5. Earl D. Wilson, *Steering Clear: Avoiding the Slippery Slope to Moral Failure* (Downers Grove, IL: InterVarsity Press, 2002), p. 158.

6. Ibid.

7. Oates, *Temptation: A Biblical and Psychological Approach,* p. 18.

8. For more info on the Harry Truman story, read Mary Ann Woolsey, ed., *The Legend of Harry Truman* (Lubbock, TX: C.F. Boone, 1981), pp. 7-8.

9. Desmond Tutu, Mpho A. Tutu and Douglas Carlton Abrams, *Made for Goodness: And Why This Makes All the Difference* (New York: HarperOne, 2010), p. 133.

10. "White Dies at 43," Sports Illustrated, December 26, 2004. http://sportsillus trated.cnn.com/2004/football/nfl/12/26/bc.fbp.lgns.reggiewhitedies.r/.

11. Jessie L. Bonner, "Idaho Couple's Dream Home Was Infested with Snakes," *Seattle Post-Intelligencer*, June 16, 2011. http://www.seattlepi.com/news/article/ Idaho-house-infested-with-snakes-ex-residents-say-1424723.php.

12. John Ortberg, *The Life You've Always Wanted: Spiritual Disciplines for Ordinary People* (Grand Rapids, MI: Zondervan, 2002), pp. 180,184.

13. Francis Chan shared this story as a guest speaker at the 2010 North American Christian Convention held on July 6-9, 2010, in Indianapolis, Indiana.

14. Clarence W. Hall, "The Village that Lived by the Bible," *Together* magazine, October 1960.

## Chapter 3: God Has an App to Break Down the Walls that Divide

1. "Favoritism," Dictionary.com. http://dictionary.reference.com/browse/fa voritism.

2. Fay Reynolds, "Psalm 23—Everything We Need," Women in Focus. http:// www.womeninfocus.org/ Psalm_23_Study.pdf.

3. "Prejudice," Dictionary.com. http://dictionary.reference.com/browse/prejudice

4. Jeremy Ball, "The Atlantic Slave Trade," National Center for History in the Schools, University of California, Los Angeles. http://www.learner.org/ courses/amerhistory/pdf/AtlanticSlaveTrade_LOne.pdf.

5. "Frequently Asked Questions About the Armenian Genocide," Armenian National Institute. http://www.armenian-genocide.org/genocidefaq.html# How_many.

6. "A Teacher's Guide to the Holocaust: Victims," University of South Florida, 2005. http://fcit.usf.edu/HOLOCAUST/people/victims.htm.

7. Tim Holden, U.S. Representative of Pennsylvania, speech delivered to the House of Representatives on the Commemoration of Holocaust Remembrance Day, April 22, 2004, Washington, DC. http://www.votesmart.org/ speech_detail.php?sc_id=119211&keyword=&phrase=&contain=.

8. "Are Dogs Color Blind?" DogTime. http://dogtime.com/dogs-colorblind-staff-faq.html.
9. Francine Brokaw, "Who Is Clark Rockefeller? TV Movie," Prime Time TV, February 28, 2010. http://www.suite101.com/content/who-is-clark-rockefeller-tv-movie-a205511.
10. "Christian Gerhartsreiter," Wikipedia.org. http://en.wikipedia.org/wiki/Christian_Gerhartsreiter.
11. Michelle Singletary, "To Truly Become Rich, You Need to Stop Acting Like It," *The Washington Post,* January 31, 2010. http://www.washingtonpost.com/wp-dyn/content/article/2010/01/30/AR2010013000031_2.html.
12. Tania Daniels, "Jesse Tree—Seeing Others Through God's Eyes," *Charleston Examiner*, December 11, 2010. http://www.examiner.com/missionary-in-charleston-sc/jesse-tree-seeing-others-through-god-s-eyes.
13. "A List of the 613 Misvot (Commandments)," Judaism 101. http://www.jewfaq.org/613.htm.

**Chapter 4: God Has an App to Resuscitate a Dying Faith**

1. "Jose Canseco Uses Brother in His Place," ESPN, March 28, 2011. http://sports.espn.go.com/sports/boxing/news/story?id=6265329.
2. Edmund Burke, *Reflections on the Revolution in France,* 1790.
3. Dietrich Bonhoeffer, *The Cost of Discipleship* (New York: Macmillan, 1960), p. 42.
4. Their website is www.venganza.org.
5. For more information about the word "faith" (Greek *pistis*) and the different ways in which the New Testament authors used the word, see Gerhard Kittel and Gerhard Friedrich (eds.) and Geoffrey W. Bromiley (trans.), *Theological Dictionary of the New Testament Abridged in One Volume* (Grand Rapids, MI: W.B. Eerdmans, 1995), pp. 853-857.
6. To read more about patron and client relationships, as well as the economic conditions of the ancient world, see Eric C. Stewart, "Social Stratification and Patronage in Ancient Mediterranean Societies"; in Dietmar Neufeld and Richard E. DeMaris (eds.), *Understanding the Social World of the New Testament* (New York: Routledge, 2010) pp. 156-166; and Alicia Batten, "The Patron-Client Institution," in Jerome H. Neyrey and Eric C. Stewart (eds.), *The Social World of the New Testament* (Peabody, MA: Hendrickson, 2008), pp. 47-62.
7. The tense of the verbs in the phrase "keep warm and well fed" is present passive imperative, which indicates that it has been said before and said again and again. See James B. Adamson, "The Epistle of James," in *The New International Commentary of the New Testament* (Grand Rapids, MI: William B. Eerdmans, 1976), p. 123.
8. Rich Mullins, "Screen Door," *Pictures in the Sky*, © 1993, Reunion.
9. *Shema* is Hebrew for "hear," the first word of Deuteronomy 6:4.

10. b. Ber. 13b (Babylonian Talmud) states, "Whoever prolongs the word *ekhad* ["one"], has his days and years prolonged." Erik Waaler, *The Shema and The First Commandment in First Corinthians: An Intertextual Approach to Paul's Re-reading of Deuteronomy* (Tübingen, Germany: Mohr Siebeck, 2008), p. 130, n. 38.

11. See Deuteronomy 6:13; 10:12; Joshua 24:14; 1 Samuel 12:24; Psalm 19:9; 33:8; Proverbs 14:11; 2 Corinthians 5:11 and Revelation 15:4, for just a few of the Scriptures that mention the fear of the Lord.

12. Visit www.bibleinayearapp.com for more information.

13. Corrie ten Boom, *The Hiding Place* (New York: Bantam, 1971), p. 238.

14. Robert H. Stein, *A Basic Guide to Interpreting the Bible: Playing by the Rules* (Grand Rapids, MI: Baker Books, 1994), p. 151.

## Chapter 5: God Has an App to Curb Your Profanity

1. Jim Labriola, quoted in Josephine Vivaldo, "Comedian Abandons Profanity for Christ," The Christian Post, June 10, 2011. http://www.christianpost.com/news/comedian-abandons-profanity-for-christ-51050/.

2. Nikita Sergeevich Khrushchev, Serge Khrushchev, George Shriver and Stephen Shenfield, *Memoirs of Nikita Khrushchev: Statesman, 1953-1964* (University Park, PA: Penn State Press, 2007), p. 893.

3. James Stuart Olson, *Historical Dictionary of the 1950s* (Westport, CT: Greenwood Publishing Group, 2000), p. 157.

4. "Tetraodontidae," Wikipedia.org. http://en.wikipedia.org/wiki/Puffer_fish.

5. "Garbage In, Garbage Out," Wikipedia. http://en.wikipedia.org/wiki/Garbage_In,_Garbage_Out.

6. Richard Foster, *Celebration of Discipline* (San Francisco: Harper & Row, 1978), p. 94.

7. Jim Collins, *Good to Great: Why Some Companies Make the Leap . . . and Others Don't* (New York: HarperCollins, 2001), pp. 23-25.

8. Spiros Zodhiates, *The Complete Word Study Dictionary: New Testament* (Chattanooga, TN: AMG Publishers, 2000).

9. Paul Tough, "Going Big: Act One—Harlem Renaissance," *This American Life,* September 26, 2008, Public Radio International. http://www.thisamericanlife.org/radio-archives/episode/364/going-big.

## Chapter 6: God Has an App to Restore a Broken Heart

1. Kyle James, "The Town that Sibling Rivalry Built, and Divided," Deutsche Welle, July 3, 2006. http://www.dw-world.de/dw/article/0,,2074427,00.html.

2. "Adidas," Wikipedia.org. http://en.wikipedia.org/wiki/Adidas.

3. "Adi/Rudi Dassler," *The Independent.* http://www.independent.co.uk/news/people/news/voight-vs-jolie-is-hollywoods-most-famous-family-feud-near-an-end-1819579.html?action=Gallery&ino=3.

4. James, "The Town that Sibling Rivalry Built, and Divided."

5. "Expanded Homicide Data," U.S. Department of Justice, 2009 data. http://www2.fbi.gov/ucr/cius2009/offenses/expanded_information/homicide.html.
6. Larry Bryant and Lesa Anne Bryant, "Shopping List," Copyright © 1984 Stonebrook Music Company (SESAC) (adm. at EMICMGPublishing.com). All rights reserved Used by permission.
7. "Friend," Dictionary.com. http://dictionary.reference.com/browse/friend.
8. Jacob and Wilhelm Grimm, "Little Snow White," from *Children's and Household Tales—Grimm's Fairy Tales* (Berlin, 1857), no. 53. http://www.pitt.edu/~dash/grimm053.html.
9. "Contrite," Dictionary.com. http://dictionary.reference.com/browse/contrite.
10. Charles F. Stanley, "Letting Go of Anger," InTouch Ministries. http://www.intouch.org/magazine/content/topic/surviving_in_an_angry_world.
11. "Clamor," Dictionary.com. http://dictionary.reference.com/browse/clamor.
12. Aesop, "The Man, the Boy, and the Donkey." http://www.aesopfables.com/cgi/aesop1.cgi?sel&TheMantheBoyandtheDonkey.

## Chapter 7: God Has an App to Prioritize Your Investments

1. For the full story, see http://www.online-literature.com/tolstoy/2738/.
2. Nigel Barley, *Grave Matters: A Lively History of Death Around the World* (New York: Henry Holt & Company, 1997), p. 84.
3. This figure is from 2006. You can see the full chart at http://pubdb3.census.gov/macro/032006/perinc/new03_001.htm.
4. This figure is from 2007. You can read the accompanying article at http://www.boston.com/news/world/articles/2007/10/07/average_earnings_worldwide/.
5. John Piper, *Don't Waste Your Life* (Wheaton, IL: Crossway Books, 2003), p. 12.
6. For more information on the life of the merchant, see David P. Nystrom, *James: NIV Application Commentary* (Grand Rapids, MI: Zondervan, 1997), pp. 250-257.
7. Timothy J. Keller, *Counterfeit Gods* (New York: Dutton, 2009), pp. ix-x.
8. Ibid., p. 52.
9. You can read his interview with ESPN at http://sports.espn.go.com/ncf/columns/story?id=6575499.
10. Read the full story at http://sports.espn.go.com/ncaa/highschool/news/story?id=6180469.
11. Randy Alcorn, *Heaven* (Wheaton, IL: Tyndale House Publishers, 2004), p. xxi.
12. You can watch the play and get commentary on the Trent Tucker Rule at http://www.youtube.com/watch?v=q99sL_g3jvo.
13. Harry Emerson Fosdick, *On Being a Real Person* (New York: Harper & Brothers, 1943), p. 84.
14. To learn more about William Borden's life, see Mrs. Howard Taylor, *Borden of Yale '09* (Philadelphia, PA: China Inland Mission, 1926).

## Chapter 8: God Has an App to Heal Your Affliction

1. "Affliction," Dictionary.com. http://dictionary.reference.com/browse/affliction.
2. "Summary Health Statistics for U.S. Adults: National Health Interview Survey, 2009," U.S. Department of Health and Human Services, series 10, no. 249, December 2010. http://www.cdc.gov/nchs/data/series/sr_10/sr10_249.pdf.
3. Jenny Wilson, "Nun Stuck in Elevator Survives Four Nights on Celery Sticks, Water and Cough Drops," *TIME*, April 2011. http://newsfeed.time.com/2011/04/28/nun-stuck-in-elevator-survives-four-nights-on-celery-sticks-water-and-cough-drops/#ixzz1S1VafTH3.
4. "Cavalry," Dictionary.com. http://dictionary.reference.com/browse/cavalry.
5. "Pastor Healed of Prostate Cancer," PreachingToday.com, August 2009. http://www.preachingtoday.com/illustrations/2009/august/3080309.html.
6. James L. Garlow and Carol Jane Garlow, *God Still Heals* (Indianapolis, IN: Wesleyan Publishing House, 2005), pp. 34-36. Used by permission.
7. Ralph Harris, *The New Testament Study Bible: Hebrews–Jude* (Springfield, MO: The Complete Biblical Library, 1989), p. 246.
8. Gary Holloway, *The College Press NIV Commentary: James and Jude* (Joplin, MO: College Press Publishing, 1996), pp. 126-127.
9. "Twin Towers Correctional Facility," Wikipedia.org. http://en.wikipedia.org/wiki/Twin_Towers_ Correctional_Facility.

# YOU CAN DOWNLOAD MORE FROM DUDLEY RUTHERFORD...

## ON YOUR  SMARTPHONE

By visiting the "app marketplace" within your Smartphone, simply type in the key words, "Call On Jesus," in the search field to purchase an awesome app that will enrich your spiritual growth in the following ways:

- Video sermons by Dudley Rutherford and other speakers, delivered straight to your phone
- 365-day devotional, Romancing Royalty, reader
- Bible In A Year reader, which includes a weekly devotional video from Dudley Rutherford.

Available through most AT&T, Sprint, Verizon Wireless, T-Mobile, or Alltel Smartphones.

## ON THE  WEB

You can also catch Dudley Rutherford's weekend messages via live streaming video during the service times mentioned below (PST) or archived messages by visiting www.DudleyRutherford.com. This site also has great resources to strengthen your walk with Christ, such as books, CD and DVD message series, articles, videos, and more!

Learn more about Dudley—including radio and television times and other ministries in which he is involved—by visiting www.DudleyRutherford.com. Or, connect with Dudley on Facebook at www.facebook.com/pastordudley and Twitter at www.twitter.com/pastordudley.

## IN  PERSON

If you're in the Los Angeles area, please visit our church, Shepherd of the Hills! Our weekend service times are Saturday at 5:00 pm and 6:30 pm, and Sunday at 8:30 am, 10:00 am, and 11:30 am. Go to www.theshepherd.org for more information.

## IN  PRINT — Available at DudleyRutherford.com

*Unleashed* – A collaborative effort by Dudley Rutherford, Francis Chan, Dave Stone, Mike Breaux and five other dynamic pastors and authors, this book challenges the status quo of Christianity in modern America. By examining the bold and effective New Testament Church, you will be inspired to turn the world upside and make a lasting impact for Jesus and the Kingdom of God—just as the early believers did!

*Romancing Royalty* – A daily devotional book designed to draw you closer to King Jesus with 365 inspirational stories, Scriptures, prayers, study questions, and place to journal. More than 100 contributors, including Greg Laurie, Coach John Wooden, Tony Campolo, Raul Ries, and Jim Garlow!

*Proverbs in a Haystack* – Now, for the first time all the treasures of the book of Proverbs are yours to find easily and quickly. This book allows you to search for any proverb by simply looking up a single word, topic, or theme, and is a wonderful resource and companion for your Bible study.

# ALSO AVAILABLE...

God Has an App for That small group DVD, and study booklet — Lead your small group gathering into a deeper study of God's apps with this high-quality DVD and booklet, which include thought-provoking study questions. Also enjoy the God Has an App for That message series by Dudley Rutherford on CD or DVD.

Visit www.GodHasAnApp.com to order your copies today!